William Herbert Thomas

Poems of Cornwall

William Herbert Thomas

Poems of Cornwall

ISBN/EAN: 9783337017422

Printed in Europe, USA, Canada, Australia, Japan

Cover: Foto ©Thomas Meinert / pixelio.de

More available books at **www.hansebooks.com**

POEMS
OF
CORNWALL
BY
THIRTY CORNISH AUTHORS;

EDITED BY
W. HERBERT THOMAS.

ALL RIGHTS RESERVED.

PENZANCE:
PRINTED AND PUBLISHED BY F. RODDA.
1892.

Price 1s. 0d. net, Post Free 1s. 0d.

THE CHANTRY OWL,
And other Poems,
By Henry Sewell Stokes.
Longmans, Green, & Co.

PHAON AND SAPPHO, and NIMROD;
Two Dramas,
By James Dryden Hosken.
Macmillan & Co. Price 5/-

MORMON SAINTS;
An Outsider's Sketch of Polygamous Life in Salt Lake City,
By W. Herbert Thomas.
Houlston & Sons. Price 1/- 200 pages.

DEEP DOWN IN A MINE,
And other Sketches in Verse,
By Richard Hambly.
Heard & Sons, Truro. Price 1/6.

CORNISH FOLKLORE,
By Miss M. A. Courtney.
Price 7/6.

LYRA CHRISTI,
Sacred and other Poems,
By Charles Lawrence Ford, B.A.
Houlston & Sons. Price 3/6.

THE SOCIALIST'S LONGING,
And other Poems,
By W. Herbert Thomas.
F. Rodda, Penzance. Price 1/-

PREFACE

HIS book is the result of a co-operative effort on the part of the authors to issue a representative volume of Cornish Poetry.

We trust it will be deemed worthy of a wide circulation, not only among Cornish people at home and abroad, but among those of the British public who are familiar with the "rocky land of strangers," and would like to carry back to crowded cities something to remind them of our hills and valleys and sunny shores, and the life of the mining, seafaring, and other dwellers in "West Barbary."

We also hope a desire will be created for the publication of some of the greater efforts of the authors in separate volumes.

All we ask of the critic is, that he will deign to notice us; and of the public, that they will read the book through rosy spectacles.

W. HERBERT THOMAS.

PENZANCE,
　July, 1892.

THE AUTHORS.

Henry Sewell Stokes, the venerable *Clerk of the Peace* and *Clerk of the Cornwall County Council*, resides at Bodmin. Mr. Worth publishes many of the poems of Mr. Stokes; Longfellow still more in his "*Poems of Places*" (of which Messrs. Macmillan & Co. hold the copyright); and Mr. Stokes has a new edition of some of his pieces ready for publication by Longmans. He has kindly permitted us to give three of his short poems in this collection. His "*Chantry Owl*," and other poems, are well-known outside of Cornwall. He is a friend of the Laureate.

A. T. Quiller-Couch, so well, and favourably, known by his initial "Q," comes of a prominent literary Cornish family. His grandfather, Jonathan Couch, was the *author of* "*A History of British Fishes*," which is still an authoritative work on the subject. His father, Thomas Quiller-Couch, was an antiquary, and the compiler of several valuable glossaries of the Cornish dialect; while his uncle, Richard Couch, achieved success in the same field. "Q" was educated at Clifton, and Trinity College, Oxford, where he wrote the poems we now publish. He particularly excels in short, quaint, dramatic and humorous stories; and has published "*Dead Man's Rock*" and several other popular books.

J. G. Ashworth, *Schoolmaster*, Perranzabuloe, Truro, is also a Wesleyan local preacher, and a contributor of poetry and prose to "*Great Thoughts*" and other periodicals.

Emra Holmes, F.R.H.S., *Collector of Customs*, Limerick, was for several years stationed at Fowey, Cornwall, and has long contributed poems to Cornish papers. He has also written stories which have appeared in magazines.

William Dale, J.P., *Draper*, Helston, published a book of poems when he was little more than a lad, from which the poems in this book have been selected. Mr. Dale is an alderman of the town council.

Miss M. A. Courtney, of Penzance, has published a book on "*Cornish Folklore*," which is a useful addition to the literature of Cornwall.

John Harris, deceased, of Falmouth, was *a Cornish miner*, known during the later years of his life (1820 to 1884) as "the Cornish Poet." He published 17 volumes of his poems, of which several thousand copies were sold. He became town missionary at Falmouth. Longfellow wrote him—"Your poems are hailed with universal applause." In 1864 he won a gold watch for his "*Ode on the Tercentenary of Shakespeare's Birthday*."

James Howard Harris, eldest and only surviving son of John Harris, is the *Master of the Board School*, Porthleven. He has written a Memoir of his deceased father; is *joint author of* "*Porthleven*," scenes from the history of a Cornish fishing village;

THE AUTHORS.

and has contributed to the "*Review of Reviews*" and other periodicals. He was born at Troon, Camborne, in 1857.

John Alfred Harris (born 1859, died 1892) was the youngest son of John Harris. He inherited some of his father's literary gifts. He died soon after returning from America, and was buried in his father's grave at Treslothan, Camborne.

Richard Hambly, *Accountant* with Messrs. Harvey & Co., Hayle, has published a volume, "*Deep Down in a Mine*," and other poems; some dealing with Cornish life and scenery, while others are of a general character. Mr. Hambly is a prominent Wesleyan.

Miss Lina Howell, Truro, has contributed short poems to Cornish and other newspapers for several years. Miss Howell intends publishing a volume of poems, illustrated with her own sketches.

James Dryden Hosken, *Poet-Postman*, of Helston, has astonished the literary world by his Greek dramas, "*Phaon and Sappho*," and "*Nimrod*," and his lyrics. He is now only about 30 years of age, and has a number of other dramas ready for publication. Mr. Gladstone, Mr. Andrew Lang, Mr. Leonard Courtney, and other eminent men, have acknowledged the great poetic gifts of this self-taught Cornishman.

William Cock, of Tuckingmill, *Draughtsman* with Messrs. Holman Brothers, Camborne, has shown his versatility by his pencil portraits, his pulpit ability, his prose writings, and his poetic contributions to "*Great Thoughts*," and Cornish papers. He is the son of a miner, and worked under-ground for a short time, until his skill in drawing was recognised and encouraged by his present employers.

W. Herbert Thomas, *Journalist*, Penzance, is the son of a Cornish mine-smith of St. Day. For seven years a mining clerk, he was afterwards a reporter for two years on the San Francisco "*Examiner*," and is now on the staff of "*The Cornishman*." He has published "*Mormon Saints*," "*Vera Trelawney*," "*The Tolseadlum Club Lectures*," etc., and is issuing a volume of poems.

W. Ambrose Taylor is now the *Clerk of the Madron Local Board*, and was for many years Assistant Curator and Librarian of the Royal Geological Society of Cornwall at Penzance.

Rev. Professor H. Cary Shuttleworth, M.A., is the well-known Christian Socialist, of St. Nicholas Cole-Abbey, Lambeth Hill, London, who has published a little volume of his poems, entitled "*Songs*." He is of Cornish parentage.

Richard Burrow, *Bookseller*, Lemon Street, Truro, is a member of the Truro Fire-brigade, and a local preacher with the Methodist body. He is a brother of Mr. J. C. Burrow, photographer, and registrar of births, deaths, and marriages, Camborne.

R. Hewett Thomas, *Music Master*, son of Mr. R. H. Thomas, Jeweller, St. Day, was for three years a student at the Royal Academy of Music. He has written a comedy, "*The Major's Tactics*," produced at Redruth.

THE AUTHORS.

Charles L. Ford, B.A., now of Bath, was for 29 years *Master of Homefield House School* at Camborne. His volume of sacred and general poems, entitled "*Lyra Christi*," is in its second edition. Mr. Ford has also been joint editor of some hymn books. He is the son of a well-known artist at Bath.

Miss Annie E. Argall, daughter of Mr. Frederick Argall, photographer, Truro, is still in her "teens," and her contributions to the local press are read with interest and appreciation.

Sam J. Williams, of Penzance, is a *Letter-carrier*, and received very little scholastic education. Rural walks have tended to develop his love of Nature and poetry.

E. L. T. Harris-Bickford, of Bedford House, Camborne, is the *Editor of "Bickford's Magazine*," and a prolific writer of prose and poetry, which have appeared in scores of English magazines and papers. He has been President of the International Literary Association, of which he is now Secretary.

Miss Jennie Harry is the youngest daughter of Mr. John Harry, Relieving Officer, Redruth. **Mrs. Kittie Juleff**, now resident in New Zealand, is an elder daughter of Mr. Harry.

John Pascoe, a self-cultured *Cornish miner*, was the author of many beautiful lyrics. He became decrepit, and lived in the Truro Workhouse, until taken out by Mrs. Smith, of the Star Hotel, a short time before his death.

Sam Richards, formerly of Gwennap, now of Redruth, is a young *Cornish miner*, who has gained a large number of science prizes.

H. D. Lowry, son of Mr. T. S. Lowry, bank manager, Camborne, has written several striking and dramatic Cornish stories, published in "*Chambers' Journal*," "*National Observer*," and elsewhere.

Miss Annie Trevithick is the daughter of Mr. William Trevithick, St. Day.

Sir Humphry Davy, as everybody knows, was the great Cornish scientist, who invented, among other things, the Davy Safety-lamp, which has been a life-preserver to the coal miner.

Miss Lena Jory lives at Lanner, near Redruth.

W. F. Woodfield, of Penzance, *Serpentine Worker*, is now in Australia.

J. F. Tiddy, *Commission Agent*, of Gwinear, formerly of Truro and St. Ives, is the *author of "Echoes from the Book of Nature.*"

Miss Amy Owen Good, a visitor to the Lizard, wrote her pretty sonnet at that picturesque health resort.

J. Jenkin, *Stationer*, Redruth, edited "*The Cornubian*" for many years.

Rev. R. S. Hawker, *Vicar of Morwenstow*, is the author of many fine poems.

Thomas Cornish, deceased, was a Lawyer, County Court Registrar, President of Penzance Antiquarian Society, etc.

William Quintrell is a *Letter-carrier*, of Camborne.

George Bown Millett, *Surgeon*, Penzance, holds important offices, and has written valuable works.

CONTENTS

	PAGES.
INTRODUCTORY : All Hail ! Old Cornwall!	1 to 4
H. S. STOKES. The Response of Earth to Heaven. Life. The Casts	5 to 7
"Q." (A. T. QUILLER-COUCH). In a College Garden. The Splendid Spur. Tim the Dragoon. Kenmare River. Titania. Retrospectoni	8 to 15
J. G. ASHWORTH. Men the Workers. To my Child. A Winter Scene. A Vision. The White Flag. Sabbath Eve. . .	16 to 24
EMRA HOLMES In Youth and Age. Autumn Thoughts. "And there shall be no more Sea." Petrarch and Laura. Cloudland. Inconstant : A Retrospect	25 to 31
WILLIAM DALE. Beauty. The Land's End. Rabbi Bonum Est. The Wreck of "The Three Brothers."	32 to 38
Miss M. A. COURTNEY. The White Ladie. Three Days .	39 to 46
JOHN HARRIS. An Ode to Shakspeare. My Last Lay. Monro .	47 to 50
J. HOWARD HARRIS. A Cornish Welcome. Woven Fancies .	50 & 51
JOHN ALFRED HARRIS. Lay of the Bereaved . . .	52 & 53
RICHARD HAMBLY. Our Sand-hills. Mount's Bay. What the Round Shell Says. Music. "The Next Thing." "God Bless You." Love. I'm Tired	54 to 61
Miss LINA HOWELL. Canzonet. Told by the Bells. Tokens. Miserere Domine	62 to 68
JAMES DRYDEN HOSKEN. Phaon and Sappho. Song. Destiny. A Day in Spring. The Order of the World. A Memory of Love. Love and Earth's Echoes. A Lover's Meditation to his Lady. Genius and Love	69 to 75
WILLIAM COCK. Thoughts from the Birds. Failed. Summer. The Swan Song. To Cornubia. "As Thou Wilt." Henry Ward Beecher. In Longfellow's Garden. In Memoriam .	76 to 83
W. HERBERT THOMAS. The Two Wishes. The Heavenly Messenger. A Song of Venice. Shadows. Battling with Clouds. The Goddess of Fashion. An Epitaph . .	84 to 91

CONTENTS.

	PAGES.
AMBROSE TAYLOR. The Granite Cliffs at the Land's End. Tolling Out the Old Year and Ringing in the New. Little Nell.	92 to 98
H. CARY SHUTTLEWORTH. Christmas Dreams. Cradle Song. My Love Loves Me. A Christmas Card. Poppies among the Corn	99 to 103
RICHARD BURROW. Wreckers and Rescuers. Voices	104 to 110
R. HEWETT THOMAS Music. The Savant. Love. Beauty. Beethoven. The Tournament	111 to 115
CHARLES LAWRENCE FORD. Resolution. The Iceberg. Pupilage Souvenirs. Life	116 to 122
Miss ANNIE F. ARGALL. Wild Flowers. The Flower-star of the Spring. A Convict's Baby. Chrysanthemums. Our Sweet English Rhine—The Fal. Our Rocky Cornish Coast	123 to 128
SAM J. WILLIAMS. Raise the Flag of Resolution. The Golden Age. The Blind Boy's Lament. A Song of Labour. Go Feed the Birds. Through Meadows Green	129 to 134
E. L. T. HARRIS-BICKFORD. Lander's Grave. When Mother's Smile was Lost to Me. Burns. When I No More. The Student's Appeal to Art	135 to 139
Miss JENNIE HARRY. Harvest Thanks. Hope	140 to 142
Mrs. KITTIE JULEFF. The Setting Sun. To my Friend. Childhood	142 to 144
JOHN PASCOE. Penseroso	145 to 147
SAM RICHARDS. Footsteps of Spring	148 & 149
H. D. LOWRY. April Night. The Gorse	149 & 150
Miss ANNIE TREVITHICK. The Golden Rule. Love's Thoughts	150 & 151
Sir HUMPHRY DAVY. St. Michael's Mount	152
Miss LENA JORY. Sing, sing, ye Waves, a Requiem !	153
W. F. WOODFIELD Money : the Modern Idol. The Emigrant's Farewell to Mount's Bay	153 & 154
J. F. TIDDY. The Lake of Killarney	155
Miss AMY OWEN GOOD. The Lizard : an English Lane	156
J. JENKIN. Gone	157
Rev. R. S. HAWKER. The Silent Tower of Bottreaux	158 & 159
THOMAS CORNISH. Sing, Birdie, Sing	159
WILLIAM QUINTRELL. The Smiling Month of May	160
GEORGE B. MILLETT. The Mayor of Market Jew. The Zennor Mermaid. Paul Churchtown	161 to 168

ALL HAIL! OLD CORNWALL!

"The rocky land of strangers."—NORDEN.

O CORNWALL! rocky land where "strangers" dwell,
   Thy scenes inspire and cheer thy favour'd sons,
From Land's End, where the echoing breakers swell,
   To where the Tamar's placid river runs;
And o'er wild oceans, in remotest lands,
   The exiled ones who hold thy memory dear,
Would link with us in love, by clasping hands,
   And swell the chanting of thy praises here!

Among thy verdant glens the winding streams
   Dance joyously, with sunny smiles illum'd;
And lovers wander, wrapp'd in fairy dreams,
   Beneath the trees with clust'ring foliage plumed:
The lark mounts high amid pellucid air,
   O'er valleys nestling 'neath the tow'ring hills,
And pours aloft a flood of music rare,
   As pure as pearly dew which earth distils.

Around thy rocky shores the billows break
   In gentle emerald curves on sand and shell;
Or caverns' groans and muffled roar awake—
   The sailors' requiem and funeral knell.
Along the beetling cliffs Time's fierce assaults
   Have sear'd and hollow'd their resisting base;
But till the circling world God's herald halts,
   No power thy majesty shall dare efface!

O Cornwall! On the scroll of history
   Thy name is writ in ancient characters,
Until we reach the veil of mystery,
   Where truth is hid, and speculation errs.
Aggressive nations cross'd the watery main
   To claim thy min'ral treasure for their prize;
And bloody battle-fields, and warriors slain,
   Awoke exultant shouts and heart-wrung cries.

Trace back a thousand years—yea, thousands more,
   And there we learn from legends that thy fame
Drew bold Phœnicians from the Spanish shore,
   And warlike Greek and Roman later came.
Perchance the metals from thy murky mines
   Adorn'd the temple rear'd by Solomon,—
That Eastern sage whose crystal wisdom shines,
   Though crumbling ruins mark the glory gone!

Still toil thy hardy miners for the tin
   By Nature stor'd within her bowels deep;
With rolling waves o'erhead,† and pent within
   The heated ground, half-naked heroes creep.
Death's shadowy form stalks, silent, as they swing
   The hewing pick, with arms like iron bars;
To quiv'ring threads of life they fearless cling,
   'Twixt hollow Earth and Heaven's eternal stars!

---

† At Levant Mine, St. Just, the hot subterranean levels, with a temperature of 100 degrees, extend three-quarters of a mile from shore under the Atlantic ocean.

And gallant seamen skirt thy storm-swept shore,
    Nor fear the tempest's wrath or lightning's flash,
As in their tiny barques they scud before
    The sobbing wind, while waters fiercely dash.
Mark how the silver fishes writhe and gleam,
    Within the meshes caught,—a harvest rare !
Thy fisher sons, how joyous now they seem,
    As shouts and merry laughter fill the air !

In golden fields, where waves the ripen'd corn,
    The husbandmen wield scythes or bind the sheaves :
How light their hearts when filling Plenty's horn ;
    When crops are blighted, how each spirit grieves !
Thy marts are throng'd, and Trade's deep hum is heard ;
    Thy artisans ply busily their tools ;
Thy halls with learning and with work are stirr'd,
    From council chambers to the children's schools.

And now, O Cornwall, think of those bright names
    In Science, Art, and Literature enrolled,—
Thy giants who, unmov'd by flood or flames,
    Their life's work wrought, their stirring message told !
Fell Superstition fled before their march ;
    Light dawn'd, and stream'd into our waiting minds ;
They rear'd o'er Beauty's shrine a rainbow arch,
    And fadeless laurel now each forehead binds !

Look now, proud Cornwall, o'er the surging sea !
    Behold the footprints traced on foreign soil !
In every land where thriveth Freedom's tree,
    Thy wand'ring sons still roam and bravely toil !
They delve for gems to deck a monarch's crown ;
    They strive for bread to feed their cherish'd ones ;
Pray God, they never may stoop basely down
    To shame, which noble manhood ever shuns !

Join hands, ye Cornish lads, across the main !
    Let Asia clasp Columbia's outstretch'd hand !
Come forth, Australia ! Swell the glad refrain !
    And touch the fringe of Afric's golden strand !
Swift o'er the boundless ocean rings the call !
    The mystic girdle round the world is cast !
Shout now with thund'rous voices " One and All " !
    All hail ! Old Cornwall ! May thy glory last !

W. HERBERT THOMAS.

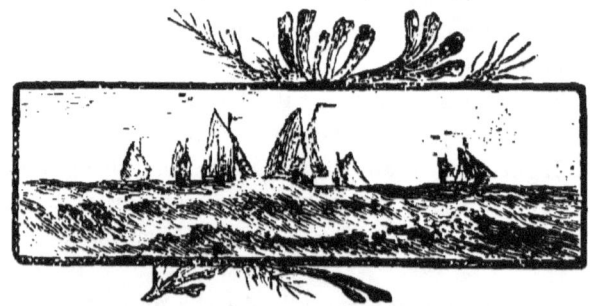

H. S. STOKES.

The Response of Earth to Heaven.

"GLORY to God on high!"
  Pealed in the starry sky;
    In softer accents then,
  While gleam'd the eternal fires,
  Sang the angelic choirs
    "Peace, and goodwill to men!"

And this the answer given
By the dark Earth to Heaven,
    "To arms! to arms! to arms!"
Nor was it long deferr'd,
And still each morn are heard
    The trumpet's shrill alarms.

And to a merry tune,
As in a gay saloon,
    Men lightly step to death;
Some bound o'er yawning waves,
Some march to grassy graves,
    And sing with their last breath.

But when the cannon booms
The ravens shake their plumes,
  The ghoul-like vultures scream;
And soon the crashing bones,
The mortal shrieks and groans,
  Dispel the soldier's dream.

Yet still the nations fight,
Heedless of wrong or right,
  Willing, or blindly driven;
Blood saturates the plain,
Blood dyes the azure main,
  And almost sprinkles Heaven.

"Glory to God on high!"
Resounds the starry sky;
  "Peace on the earth!" but when?
Not till the world grows wise,
And all the people rise
  And say Amen! Amen!

Life.

I.

DESCRIBE me life. A blossom'd thorn,
A poppy waving in the corn,
Waiting the silent reaper's thrust,—
A bubble's shadow, dreams and dust.

II.

Give me some other similes,
The thistle-down before the breeze,
A leaf, a flower, a bead of dew,
A gossamer—what more would you?

III.

Your fancy's fertile—try again.
'Tis a steed bounding on the plain,
'Tis a sail scudding from the strand,
A bird, a wave, a drift of sand.

IV.

Can you no other symbols find?
A cadence wafted on the wind,
The fitful breathing of a shell,
The echo of a plaintive bell.

The Casts.

I.

Casts were they of the features fine
Of wise and good and honour'd men;
But soon the damps effaced each line,
And they were lumps of clay again.
So did the living forms decay,
And turn into their native clay;
But why so much the Casts deplore,
If God will their lost moulds restore?

II.

Will He? You preach it, and believe,
And let my faith your creed sustain,
That the dear friends for whom we grieve
Still link'd with us by love remain:
The looks, the smiles, the tones we miss,
The hallow'd sweetness of the kiss,
The warmth of hand and heart I never
Can believe lost, and lost for ever.

III.

And thinking of their pains and cares,
So bravely met, so meekly borne,
Their tears and sighs, and secret prayers,
Their tenderness, did others mourn;
Their patient toil, their earnest thought,
Their wisdom by hard lessons bought,
Their lofty hopes, their filial trust
In God—I feel they are not dust.

"Q."

(A. T. QUILLER-COUCH.)

In a College Garden.

The Senior Fellow.

SAYE, cushat, callynge from the brake,
  What ayles thee soe to pyne?
Thy carefulle heart shall cease to ache
  When dayes be fyne
  And greene thynges twyne:
Saye, cushat, what thy griefe to myne?

The Dove.

Naye, gossyp, loyterynge soe late,
  What ayles thee thus to chyde?
My love is fled by garden-gate;
  Since Lammas-tyde
  I wayte my bryde:
Saye, gossyp, whom dost thou abyde?

The Senior Fellow.

Loe! I am he, the Lonelie Man,
  Of Time forgotten quite,
That no remember'd face may scanne—
  Sadde eremyte,
  I wayte to-nyghte,
Pale Death, nor any other wyghte.

O, cushat, cushat, callynge lowe,
  Goe waken Time from sleepe:
Goe whysper in his ear, that soe
    His besom sweepe
    Me to that heape
Where all my recollections keepe.

Hath he forgott? Or did I viewe
  A ghostlye companye
This even, by the dismalle yewe,
    Of faces three
    That beckoned me
To land where no repynynges be?

O, Harrye, Harrye, Tom and Dicke,
  Each lost companion!
Why loyter I among the quicke
    When ye are gone?
    Shall I alone
Delayinge cry "Anon, Anon?"

Naye, let the spyder have my gowne,
  To brayde therein her veste.
My cappe shal serve, now I goe down,
    For mouse's nest.
    Loe! this is best.
I care not, soe I gayne my reste.

The Splendid Spur.

Not on the neck of prince or hound,
  Nor on a woman's finger twin'd,
May gold from the deriding ground
  Keep sacred that we sacred bind:
      Only the heel
      Of splendid steel
  Shall stand secure on sliding fate,
  When golden navies weep their freight.

The scarlet hat, the laurell'd stave
   Are measures, not the springs, of worth ;
In a wife's lap as in a grave,
   Men's airy notions mix with earth.
        Seek other spur,
        Bravely to stir
   The dust in this loud world, and tread
   A lord among the whisp'ring dead.

Trust in thyself—then spur amain !
So shall Charybdis wear a grace,
Foul Ætna laugh, the Lybian plain
Take roses to her shrivell'd face.
        This orb—this round
        Of sight and sound—
Count it the lists that God hath built
For haughty hearts to ride a-tilt.

IRISH MELODIES.

I.

Tim the Dragoon.

(From "Troy Town.")

Be aisy an' list to a chune
That's sung of bowld Tim the Dragoon—
    Sure, 'twas he'd niver miss
    To be stalin' a kiss,
Or a brace, by the light of the moon—
                Aroon—
Wid a wink at the Man in the Moon !

Rest his sowl where the daises grow thick ;
For he's gone from the land of the quick :
    But he's still makin' love
    To the leddies above,
An' be jabbers ! he'll tache 'em the thrick—
                Avick—
Niver doubt but he'll tache 'em the thrick !

'Tis by Tim the dear saints 'll set sthore,
And 'ull thrate him to whisky galore :
  For they've only to sip
  But the tip of his lip
An' bedad! they'll be askin' for more—
    Asthore—
By the powers, they'll be shoutin' "Ancore!"

II.

Kenmare River.

'Tis pretty to be in Ballinderry,
 'Tis pretty to be in Ballindoon,
But 'tis prettier far in County Kerry
 Coortin' under the bran' new moon,
    Aroon, Aroon!

'Twas there by the bosom of blue Killarney
 They came by the hundther' a-coortin' me;
Sure I was the one to give back their blarney,
 An' merry it was to be fancy-free.

But niver a step in the lot was lighter,
 An' divvle a boulder among the bhoys,
Than Phelim O'Shea, me dynamither,
 Me illigant arthist in clock-work toys.

'Twas all for love he would bring his figgers
 Of iminent statesmen, in toy machines,
An' hould me hand as he pulled the thriggers
 An' blew the thraytors to smithereens.

An' to see the Queen in her Crystial Pallas,
 Fly up to the roof, an' the windeys broke!
And all with divvle a trace of malus,—
 But he was the bhoy that enjoyed his joke!

Then O, but his cheek would flush, an' "Bridget,"
 He'd say, "Will yez love me?" But I'd be coy,
And answer him, "Arrah now, dear, don't fidget!"
 Though at heart I loved him, me arthist bhoy!

One night we stood by the Kenmare river,
  An' " Bridget, creina, now whist," said he,
" I'll be goin' to-night, an' may be for iver,
  Open your arms at the last to me."

'Twas there by the banks of the Kenmare river
  He took in his hands me white, white face,
An' we kissed our first an' our last for iver—
  For Phelim O'Shea is disparsed in space.

'Twas pretty to be by blue Killarney,
  'Twas pretty to hear the linnets' call,
But whist! for I cannot attind their blarney,
  Nor whistle in answer at all, at all.

For the voice that he swore 'ud out-call the linnet's
  Is cracked intoirely, and out of chune,
Since the clock-work missed it by thirteen minutes
  An' scattered me Phelim around the moon,
                      Aroon, Aroon!

Titania.

By Lord T———n.

So bluff Sir Leolin gave the bride away;
And when they married her, the little church
Had seldom seen a costlier ritual.
The coach and pair alone were two-pound-ten,
And two-pound-ten apiece the wedding-cakes,—
Three wedding-cakes. A Cupid poised a-top
Of each hung shivering to the frosted loves
Of two fond cushats on a field of ice,
As who should say "*I* see you!"—Such the joy
When English-hearted Edwin swore his faith
With Mariana of the Moated Grange.
For Edwin, plump head-waiter at The Cock,

Grown sick of custom, spoilt of plenitude,
Lacking the finer wit that saith, "I wait,
They come ; and if I make them wait, they go,"
Fell in a jaundiced humour, petulant-green,
Watched the dull clerk slow-rounding to his cheese,
Flicked a full dozen flies that flecked the pane—
All crystal-cheated of the fuller air,
Blurted a free "Good day t'ye," left and right,
And shaped his gathering choler to this end :—

"Custom ! And yet what profit of it at all ?
The old order changeth, yielding place to new,
To me small change, and this the counter-change
Of custom beating on the self-same bar—
Change out of chop ! Ah me ! the talk, the tip,
The would-be-evening, should-be-mourning suit,
The forged solicitude for petty wants
More petty still than they,—all these I loathe,
Learning they lie who feign that all things come
To him that waiteth. I have waited long,
And now I go, to mate me with a bride
Who is a-weary waiting, even as I !"

But when the amorous moon of honeycomb
Was over, ere the matron-flower of Love—
Step-sister of to-morrow's marmalade—
Swooned scentless, Mariana found her lord
Did something jar the nicer feminine sense
With usage, being all too fine and large,
Instinct of warmth and colour, with a trick
Of blunting "Mariana's" keener edge
To "Mary Ann"—the same, yet not the same :
Whereat she girded, tore her crispèd hair,
Called him "Sir Churl," and ever calling "Churl !"
Drave him to Science, then to Alcohol,
To forge a thousand theories of the rocks,
Then somewhat else for thousands dewy-cool
Wherewith he sought a more Pacific isle,
And there found love, a darker love than hers.

Retrospection.

WHEN the hunter-star Orion,
(Or, it may be, Charles his Wain),
Tempts the tiny elves to try on
All their little tricks again ;
When the earth is calmly breathing
Draughts of slumber undefiled,
And the sire (unused to teething)
Seeks, for errant pins, his child :

When the Moon is on the Ocean,
And our little sons and heirs,
From a natural emotion,
Wish the luminary theirs ;
Then a feeling, hard to stifle,
Even harder to define,
Makes me feel I'd give a trifle
For the days of Auld Lang Syne.

James,—for we have been as brothers,—
Are, to speak correctly, twins,
Went about in one another's
Clothing ; bore each other's sins ;
Rose together, ere the pearly
Tint of dawn had left the heaven ;
And retired (absurdly early)
Simultaneously at seven—

James, the days of yore were pleasant !
Sweet to climb for alien pears
Till the irritated peasant
Came and took us unawares ;
Sweet to devastate his chickens
As the ambushed catapult
Scattered—and the very dickens
Was the natural result :

Sweet to snare the thoughtless rabbit:
Break the next-door-neighbour's pane;
Cultivate the smoker's habit
On the not-innocuous cane;
Leave the Exercise unwritten;
Systematically cut
Morning school, to plunge the kitten
In his bath, the water-butt.

Age, my James, that from the cheek of
Beauty steals its rosy hue,
Has not left us much to speak of;
But 'tis not for *this* I rue.
Beauty with its thousand graces —
Hair and tints that will not fade,
You may get from many places
Practically ready-made.

No. It is the evanescence
Of those ruddier tints of Hope, —
Bubbles, such as adolescence
Joys to win from melted soap —
Emphasising this conclusion, —
That the dreams of youth remain
Castles that are An delusion
(Castles, that's to say, in Spain).

Time thinks fit, and I say "Fiat."
Here I stand for Fortune's butt,
As for Sunday swains to shy at,
Stands the stoic cocoa-nut.
If you wish it put succinctly,
Gone are all our little games;
But I thought I'd say distinctly
What I feel about it, James.

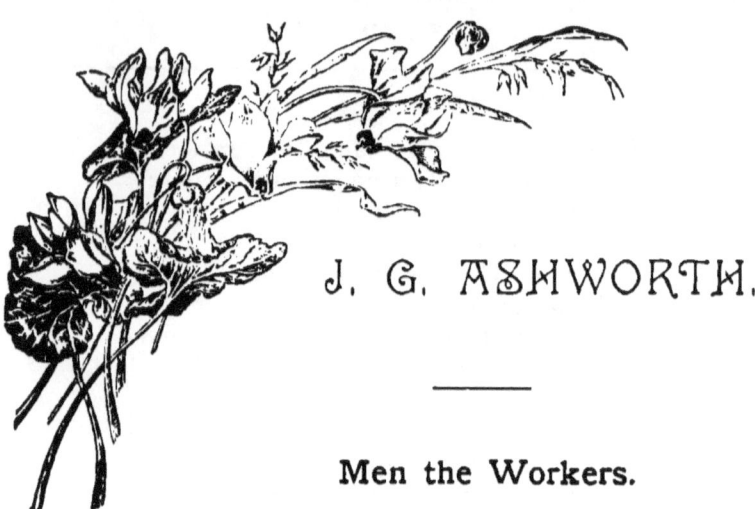

J. G. ASHWORTH.

Men the Workers.

Work, my brothers, dreams are naught,
Though with utmost splendour fraught,
If in actions ne'er out-wrought.
Those who more than others thrive
Drone not in life's busy hive,
But with giant effort strive.
Some may hold that honest trade,
Weft and shuttle, pick and spade,
And the humble plough, degrade;
Theirs alone to dine and dress—
Unambitious, purposeless—
Wasting life in idleness.
But your toil dishonours not;
So you keep your souls from blot
Kings might envy ye your lot.
Did not Adam delve the soil?
And his progeny must toil
Would they garner fruitage-spoil.
What are 'scutcheons covered o'er
With a dread heraldic lore,
Dripping daggers, hands of gore?
Your escutcheon is a shield

Bright with mountain, shop, and field,
And the tools ye deftly wield.
Ships that plough the pathless main,
Snorting engine, peopled train,
Whirling headlong o'er the plain—
Arches, bridges, churches tall,
Lordly castle, lordly hall,—
Humble workers made them all.
Work then, brothers; horny hands
Shape the future, knit the lands
With the love-electric bands.
Work, for work wrought honestly,
While it must ennoble ye,
Blesseth all humanity!

To my Child.

I.

O, my child, thy cheeks are fair!
  O, my child, thy locks are bright!
And thou knowest not the care
  That is in my heart to-night!
Blithe as bird on airy wing—
Pure thy soul as crystal spring—
Thou canst laugh and thou canst sing—
          Happy child!

II.

O, my child, to be as thou,
  I would gleefully forego
Hopes of laurel on my brow—
  And the little that I know;
I would barter manhood's prime
For a day of thy glad time
On the verge of Heaven's clime—
          Blessèd child!

III.

O, my child, the thought is vain.
   I have quaffed life's crystal draught,
I have sung my careless strain
   Till the very echoes laughed ;
Now my songs are turned to sighs,
And a grave before me lies
Under barren, winter skies—
               Ah, my child !

A Winter Scene.

I.

This morn the hills are white with snow,
   And neighbouring trees, both branch and stem,
   Wear many a pure and wondrous gem,
Whose facets sparkle in the glow

II.

Of golden sunshine.—Here and there,
   A bright cloud, bark-like, trim and free,
   Sails silent o'er its azure sea,
And all the out-look showeth fair.

III.

But beauty or of earth or sky
   Has not the charm it had of yore,
   When I could pace life's sunlit shore,
And see broad paths of splendour lie

IV.

To westward.—Glorious was it then
   To buckle on day's burnished mail,
   And forth, whatever might assail,
To play a manly part 'mong men.

V.

But change came as it comes to all,
   The broad-pathed splendours died away,
   And o'er me hung a dismal grey,
That wrapped my spirit like a pall.

VI.

And thus I once struck notes of woe;
   Singing, that under "winter skies"
   I saw a grave.—Ah, in it lies
Not, not the one I thought would go.

VII.

In sight of God's great rolling main,
   My darling in his wee cot sleeps
   Beside a swelling mound that keeps
It sheltered from the wind and rain.

VIII.

And on it now the white snow lies,
   Soft as the down on birdie's breast,
   That hovers o'er my darling's nest,
And flings its music to the skies.

A Vision.

Methought that in my slumbers yesternight
This scene tremendous rose before my sight.

Four spirits stood in front of a White Throne,
   Which arcs of perfect beauty did enfold;
"And who art thou?" said He who sat thereon,
   Unto the foremost. "I'm a warrior bold,
And my full fame to the four winds is blown."
Swift o'er the Glory, as light cloud o'er sun,
   A shadow swept. "Well, from thy youth till now
What hast thou in the world's arena done?"

A sudden gleam lit up the warrior's brow,
  "Led armies, taken cities, kingdoms won."
Sternly the Sceptred spake, "And hast thou then
Done naught but scourge thy helpless fellow men?
Pass on; thy deeds on earth may be rehearsed,
But here thou dwellest evermore accurst."

"And who art thou?" the Presence once more said,—
"A scholar in all knowledge deeply read."
"*All* knowledge! well in three score years and ten
  What didst thou to uplift thy fellow men?"
"Books were my fellows, and with them I spent
  Life's sweet seclusion in most sweet content."
Again in sternest tones the Glory spake—
"And didst thou nought for thy sad kindred's sake?
Know thou, one heart-begotten deed were more
Than all thy knowledge piléd ten times o'er.
Pass on; I gave thee life for noblest use,
And thou ignobly put it to abuse."

"And who art thou?" the dread Voice asked a sprite
  That proudly stood upon the warrior's right.
"I am a merchant prince, a millionare;
    My white-winged argoises sail every sea;
  My sons are strong, my daughters they are fair,
    And few on earth can be compared to me."
"Well," said th' Enthron'd, with look as grievéd sore,
"In all that affluent time which now is o'er,
What didst thou with thy wealth?" "I made it more."
"Didst nothing for the want-beliveried throngs
  Who near thee dwelt, crushed down by cruel wrongs?"
"Not I forsooth! what were such scum to me?"
"Man!" spake the Voice, and awful was its tone,
As thunder, crash on crash, in torrid zone.
Each seraph stood before his trembling lute
With nerveless fingers; lips, though parted, mute.
"Man, pride-swoll'n, vain, what were such scum to thee?

Such scum were dear as my own blood to me ;
And since thou hold'st my lov'd ones high in scorn,
Thou shalt be stripped, of all thy splendours shorn,
And when they laugh, thy doom shall be to mourn."

"And who art thou ?" the Rainbowed sweetly said,
Unto the fourth, who stood with drooping head.
"An unknown dweller in an obscure fen,
The lowliest and unworthiest of men."
"And didst do aught in thy brief span of years
To make thee meet for bright supernal spheres."
"My deeds were few and poor," the sprite replied,
"I lived, I loved, I laboured, and then died."
"You loved you say, and therefore, now behold !"
He looked and saw a wondrous scroll unrolled
Whereon was writ, in characters of flame,
The acts of men against each several name ;
And there his own ; and how he'd spoke and wrought
Kind words, kind deeds, the fruits of generous thought ;
And how once when afield, the sun o'erhead,
He'd fasted that a beggar might be fed.
He saw and spake,—his cheeks of crimson hue,—
"Why these were nought ; what other could I do ?"
"Come hither," said the Voice in tenderest tone,
'Tis such as thou, the Father claims His own."
And clouds of glory and exceeding light
Rolled round the swain, and hid him from my sight.

The White Flag.

Down with the flag, the blood-red flag,
  Of glory and of pride !
Beneath whose shade unnumbered men
  Like slaughtered brutes have died.
Oh ! it has waved too long, too long,
  And we have loved too well,
Nor deemed that under it have marched
  The sable hosts of hell.

Up with the fair, white flag of peace,
    And let it blow afar,
Where'er great guns have bellowed doom,
    Or howled the dogs of war.
Up with the glorious flag on high,
    And let your shouts arise,
For under it are gathering now
    The squadrons of the skies.

Down with the blood-red flag of war,
    Up with the flag of peace;
For as the rule of might grows less
    Love's empire will increase.
Up with the streamer of the skies,
    The snow-white flag I sing,
Till, aided by our bright allies,
    The Christ, the Christ is King!

Sabbath Eve.

Come, comrade, let us rest a while;
    Upon this grassy mound we'll sit,
And watch the daylight's parting smile
    Fade in the spangled infinite!

The week was wearisome and dull;
    The body worn, the brain o'erwrought;
But here, amid the beautiful,
    All pain is lost in raptured thought.

Rich in our minds, and free our souls,
    Deep-quaffing God's exhaustless air,
We envy not the wight who rolls
    In affluence which *we* may not share.

Who could behold this mountain's cope,
    Sky-lifting, bathed in mellowest sheen,
Those white-washed walls, each graceful slope
    That, wave-like, undulates between.

Nor feel some thrill, some mystic spell;
   Ay! though the veriest earth-born clod,
Would make his inmost being swell,
   Responsive to the present God?

Hark! 'tis the throstle's latest lay,
   Low brooding o'er its new built nest;
Thus may *we* end life's latest day,
   And singing, slumber into rest.

Come, comrade, chill dews fall apace,
   And dense clouds wrap the mountains round;
Gone is the grandeur and the grace,
   And misty vapours hide the ground.

'Tis thus life's fairest visions go,
   Lost in the blinding mists of grief;
And were it not for Hope's rare bow
   Could we live out life's day, though brief?

But come, for we from home are far,
   And there's an aspect in yon sky,
That tells me many a crashing jar
   Will shake heaven's concave by and by.

No doubt some will our walk condemn,
   Say retribution's in the rain;
But of God's robe we've touched the hem,
   And strengthen'd feel in heart and brain.

We've sat with nature's self to muse
   On all things bright and beauteous given,
Till highest thoughts partook their hues,
   And, rainbow-like, knit earth to heaven.

O! sure this glorious world we see,
   And that blue arch that bends above,
Speak an unmeasured Deity,
   Of boundless mercy, boundless love.

Regret.

Regret, like pale-faced nun in tears,
Has followed me for many years;
On Alpine heights, where hue on hue—
Glory on glory, met my view ;
Beside the giant pyramids
Where morning opes her dainty lids ;
Or under far Hesperian skies
Where daylight softly, sweetly dies.
No matter whither I have gone
   In all this beauteous world below,
That dark-robed shade has followed on
   With large sad eyes and face of snow.

But wherefore ? wherefore ? soul, canst say ?
Alas ! it seems but yesterday
Hot anger seized his ready bow
And winged a shaft that laid love low.
'Twas in a moment, yet an age
Can ne'er atone that moment's rage ;
It swept like fierce Sirocco's breath,
And left behind a track of death ;
And do my best—go where I will—
   In all this barren world below,
That gloomy shadow follows still
   With large sad eyes and face of snow.

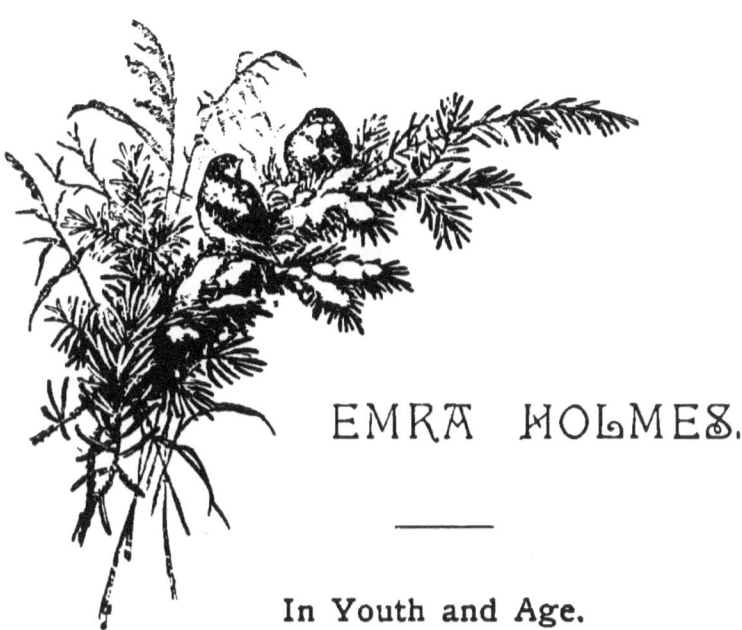

EMRA HOLMES.

In Youth and Age.

ALL through the days of May, the cuckoo calling,
    Reminds us that the Spring-tide now hath come;
And every song-bird sings, though showers are falling,
    For nature, joyous, ceases to be dumb.

In youth how pensively we love the days,
    When Autumn's sweet decay is over all;
When woods are brown and golden, and the haze
    Of dying summer seems o'er us to fall.

Though few the shadows that have crossed our path,
    We love the long drawn sigh, the soft lament;
What wrongs we lack, imagination hath;
    With fancied sorrows we are well content.

With manhood still before us, in our prime,
    We contemplate serenely Nature's death;
And love the falling leaves in Autumn time,
    Yet think but little what the preacher saith.

But when the sorrows of our life are come,
    And all the ills to which our flesh is heir ;
When Azrael hath visited our home,
    And we are tempted to a dark despair—

When age is creeping on, we pause to think ;
    To Nature's resurrection now we cling ;
Of waters of Nepenthe fain would drink ;
    We bless the rays of Hope which come with Spring.

Autumn Thoughts.

Leaves are lingering yet upon the trees,
The branches waving sadly in the breeze ;
Though glorious tints of autumn are on these,
    The shadow of decay is over all.

Bright russet tinges in the wooded dells,
Gay crimson flushes where the squirrel dwells,
And in the darksome glen, where magic spells
    Seem, like the night, on everything to fall.

Grim Winter threatens now to come apace,
And bleak East winds now do the dead leaves chase ;
November glooms are over every place,
    The frosty rime is on the poplar tall.

Soon there will come the angry bitter wind,
Rifling the forests,—with its gusts unkind—
Of all their golden leaves, but ivy twined
    O'er gnarlèd trunks lists never to the call.

The seasons come and go and all the leaves ;
The swallow gently twitters 'neath the eaves,
But Summer past, deserts us, never grieves :
    The ivy clings for ever on our wall.

The old tree dies, but still the ivy clings,
As though it were amongst the sentient things ;
And o'er the crumbling ruin bidden springs,
    Near holy wells, and where the cuckoos call.

So steadfast friend will ever through the strife,
And turmoil of our constant changing life,
Cling to us always, like true wedded wife,
   Though life be ending and all pleasures pall.

"And there shall be no more Sea."

I climbed the crest of a noble cliff that juts out into the sea
And lay me down to bask in the sun and wonder dreamily—
Why all this beautiful waste of waters, glittering in the sheen
Of the summer sun, should cease to be, as though it had never been.

The manifold changes over its face as it gleamed bright in the sun,
Whilst glorious tints of opal and gold passed over one by one;
The monotonous roll of the heaving waves as they came in from the west,
Each one with the white foam crowning it with a snowy, shimmering crest.

And listening there to the dreamy moan of the brilliant, restless sea,
Methought I heard a low sad voice speak out of its mystery :
" I am the ocean vast " it said, " grand type of eternity ;
And yet as time itself shall end so shall I soon cease to be.

" And I shall give up my dead to Him who ruleth the mighty deep ;
They have lain on my breast for centuries, I have rocked them all to sleep :
I am the mighty mother and my children all come unto me,
And they are always hushed to rest by the monotone of the sea.

"The poets call me beautiful, and the painters paint me so,
Yes, and the great philosophers measure my ebb and flow,
And wonder over my mystery and what is the moon to me:
But why we move together is the secret of the sea.

Aye, yes, 'the stately ships go on to their haven under the hill,'
But no man knoweth whether my waves, that are flowing cold and chill,
Shall cover him over, lull him to rest, far down in my depths of gloom,
Where myriads of men have found before the dread of a watery tomb.

" For the King hath said it, I know no more, only it is to be ;
His mighty fiat hath long gone forth " And there shall be no more sea ;"
Beautiful am I, passionless, yet there is no room in heaven:
To the grand majestic ocean there is no welcome given."

Petrarch and Laura.

"THE darkest hour is always before dawn,"
   So saith the olden proverb. Is it true?
Ah! love, dear love, bethink thee of this phrase,
   Nor take a step that thou must ever rue.

Be patient, for the end will surely come;
   Such love as mine must some day have reward—
Thy knightly champion I shall ever be,
   And only ask to live in thy regard.

Fate is against us now— may e'er be so ;
   I dare not yet the future seek to trace ;
But whether we shall meet again, or no,
   I never shall forget thy sweet, sad face.

When gleams of silver come upon thy hair,
    And trouble prematurely dims thine eye,
To me thou wilt be beautiful and fair
    As lovely landscape, or soft summer sky.

Though I should live to be a hundred years,
    And all my memories fade into the past;
When the death-angel comes then through my tears
    Thy name will be upon my lips the last.

"The darkest hour is always before dawn"—
    Take comfort in adversity from this;
If love shall never have requital here,
    It may have place in realms of endless bliss.

The sea of sorrow, and the gloom of death,
    May overwhelm us for a little space;
Yet, if we may not meet on earth again,
    We shall in Heaven, by Christ's saving grace.

Cloudland.

A BREAK in the clouds, and the distant sky
    Shines soft and fair in the evening light;
A glimpse of celestial realms on high,
    Seen through the canopy of night.

And they sweep along in their majesty,
    And dash themselves 'gainst the great hill side,
Then drop in tears, for their destiny
    Is only to fall in their fruitless pride.

The distant mountains are white with snow,
    Reflecting the sun's last beauteous gleam,
First burnished silver, and then with a glow
    Of roseate hue, like some sweet dream.

Battalions of clouds, like angels bright,
    Their snowy pinions and serried mass,
In the proud panoply of their might,
    As in a vision, I see them pass.

There are spectre faces, and towering forms,
    And endless shadowy shapes of fear ;
The ghastly portents of coming storms,
    That come with the sobbing winds so drear.

And then the billowy oceans vast,
    Where ghostly ships are sailing o'er,
With freight of souls, all sorrow past,
    Floating to rest on the heavenly shore.

And Alpine ranges, shadowy, dim,
    I note them towering, lofty, grand,
With little cloudlets near each rim,
    A line of light o'er a pearly strand.

And oh ! the castles high in the air ;
    The vast cathedrals, Gothic spires ;
The palaces that are so fair ;
    Methinks I hear the heavenly choirs.

A fairy vision, and wondrous sweet ;
    A picture of Heaven so far away ;
Who cannot see, and with poets greet,
    A gleam from the realm of deathless day ?

I note ye all as ye sweep along,
    Or calmly rest at peace on high ;
Yet I yearn for the sapphire vault of Heaven,
    For I love to gaze on a starlit sky.

Oh ! lovely cloudland, summer skies,
    With your soft opalescent glow ;
Ye splendid wraiths in carmine dyes,
    And tints not painter yet could show.

I love ye well, and I gladly praise
    The great Creator who made ye all ;
The clouds and the hill, the sea and the land,
    The sun to shine, and the rain to fall.

Inconstant: A Retrospect.

The turbid stream flows swift and strong,
   To pour its volume in the sea;
And by its side I stroll along:
   But what is that to you and me?

From long lush grass the corncrake calls;
   I watch but fail its form to see:
Its harsh note on my memory falls:
   But what is that to you and me;

In hidden groves the sweet birds sing—
   A year ago, down o'er the lea,
I mind me how the church bells rang:
   But what is that to you and me?

We sauntered happy, side by side;
   I spoke of love, and you were free;
You would be mine, whate'er betide:
   But what is that to you and me?

The corncrake calls again once more,
   As then I heard it; can it be
That there shall ring, for all is o'er,
   No marriage bells for you and me?

WILLIAM K. DALE.

Beauty.

She sits enthroned the stars among;
    She dances in the moonlight beam;
She trips the waving fields along,
    And glides adown the silver stream;
She sparkleth in the ocean spray,
And shineth in the morning ray!

She gives the heavens their azure hue,
    The clouds their gold and crimson dyes;
She beams in every drop of dew,
    And throws her rainbow o'er the skies;
On mount, wood, valley, river—all,
Her smiles of bright enchantment fall!

Hers are the blossomings of Spring;
    And her's the golden Autumn fruit;
We see her on the insect's wing,
    And trace her in the tenderest shoot:—
She fires the thought, she thrills the soul,
And binds the heart with sweet control.

She sporteth 'mid the Arctic snows,
    And buildeth there her crystal towers;
She roameth where the Indus flows,
    And scattereth there her saffron flowers;
She showers her gifts with frolic hand
On flaming peak and flashing strand.

Deep, deep in subterranean cave
    She sleeps, unseen by mortal eye;
Beneath the blue, transparent wave,
    Above the bright, unclouded sky:
In olive groves, and sapphire cells,—
In sea, sky, earth, and heaven, she dwells.

The Land's-End.

BATTLER with the fierce Atlantic,
    Hail! Britannia's Vanguard, hail!
Tempests wild, and billows frantic,
    O'er thee never shall prevail.
Thou art mighty! thou art peerless!
    Storm may howl, or ocean foam;
Thou art steadfast; thou art fearless;
    Firm in thy eternal home.

Thou hast waged the war of ages;
    Borne the fury of the Past;
Still the ceaseless conflict rages,—
    Thou defiest still the blast.
Still unvanquished, thou art braving
    Every charge that thunders by;
Vain the elemental raving,—
    Vain the wrath of sea and sky!

Shipwrecks, deaths, and desolations,
    Hurricanes have round thee rolled ;
Strewed about thy dark foundations
    Bales of silk and bars of gold.
Rocks majestic ! cliffs stupendous !
    Ye have heard the midnight cry ;
Hurled before the surge tremendous
    Seen the struggling sailor die.

Burns the beacon ! Brightly, beacon,
    Flash thy warning o'er the waves ;
For the mountain billows break on,
    For the fearful tempest raves !
There are brave ships on the ocean ;
    There are dear men on the deep :—
Save ! or else in mad commotion
    Hearts will break and orphans weep.

In thy caves what spoils are lying,—
    Persian pearl and Indian gem,
Bright as those that, price defying,
    Shine in princely diadem.
Loved ones fondly, dearly cherished,
    Rest beneath thy foaming wave ;
Here, a mother's hope hath perished,
    There, a father's found a grave.

Sweeps the tempest,—they are quiet ;
    Roar the billows,—calm they lie :
Hear they not the ocean's riot,
    Heed they not the whirlwind's sigh.
Oh ! methinks those caves are holy ;
    Sacred is that flinty bed ;
There they rest in slumbers lowly
    Till the sea shall yield her dead.

Battler with the fierce Atlantic,
   Hail! Britannia's Vanguard, hail!
Tempests wild, and billows frantic,
   O'er thee never shall prevail.
Thou art glorious! thou art fearless!
   Storm may howl, or ocean foam:
Thou art lone, and stern, and peerless,—
   Firm in thy eternal home!

Rabbi bonum est.

"MASTER, it is good to be,
   On the Holy Mount with Thee:
Here, O Master, grant that we
   Build Thee tabernacles three;
One for Elias let there be,
   For Moses one, and one for Thee."

Thus exclaimed the chosen Three;—
Spake the sons of Zebedee;
Ever leader of the van,
Spake the fiery fisherman;—
"Here, O Master, grant that we
   Evermore abide with Thee."

But they knew not what they said—
Hark! it thunders overhead;
Lo! the voice of Him who spoke
Shakes the mountain, rends the rock;
While the saints, in clouds of light,
Vanish from their dazzled sight.

Had they with a Seer's ken
Swept the wondrous Future then,
At their feet what scenes had lain!
Steeps of glory,—deeps of pain;
But their heavy eyes of clay
Flashed not with prophetic ray.

Saw they not their Lord and Head
Like a lamb to slaughter led;
Saw Him not in triumph risen
From the Grave's demolished prison;
Nor the cloven flame-tongues fall
On the Spirit's Festival.

Saw they not the rack, the wheel,
Scourging thong, and stabbing steel;
Heard not the mad multitude
Fiercely clamouring for their blood;
And the thronged arena ring
At the tiger's deadly spring.

Saw not Peter's death abhorred;
Saw not Hell-doomed Herod's sword
Dripping with the blood of James;
Saw they not the cauldron's flames,
Nor the island's visioned caves
Washed with wild Ægean waves.

As of old thy chosen Three,
So, O Master, now are we;
On the Mount, like them, we pray,
But we know not what we say;
For through blood, and flame, and strife,
Lies the path that leads to life.

The Wreck of the "Three Brothers."

LEAGUES, leagues south-west of Scilly,
  Drove the great Mackerel Fleet;—
They drove from dusk to daybreak,
  In spite of sea and sleet.

In spite of storm, and sea, and sleet,
  Spite of the blinding hail;
The wind grew to a hurricane
  Before they hoisted sail.

Then rose the huge Atlantic waves!
  And the great fleet, shore-wards,
Storm-foresailed, flew through scud and drift,
  Like flocks of frightened birds.

Some for St. Mary's harbour ran,
  Some for St. Michael's bay:—
O desperate was that race for life
  That dreadful April day.

Three luggers sailed in company,
  Three boats of equal speed;
Sternmost the "Triumph" dashed along;
  The "Annie" had the lead.

Meanwhile three cables' lengths between
  The good "Three Brothers" kept,
As for St. Mary's sheltered roads
  League after league they swept.

Still louder roared the hurricane,
  Still fiercer raged the sea;
And one huge billow, topmast high,
  Broke o'er the "Brothers Three!"

A minute more the "Triumph" passed
  Some nets, a keg, an oar;
Ahead, the "Annie," and a wild
  White waste of foam,—no more!

What grudge hadst thou against the boat?
  Thou cruel, greedy Sea!
Seven poor plain families stript of all,—
  What gain was that to thee?

For thee, dear friend of noble heart,
  To a rough calling bred,
For thee I will not weep,—thou art
  With the victorious dead.

Hurled by that mighty mountain wave,
    By that fierce tempest driven,
Through the black channel of the grave
    Into the blaze of Heaven.

Snatched from the sinking lugger's deck,
    Translated from the abyss;
One moment—death, destruction, wreck!
    The next—God, glory, bliss!

Memory.

The heart is like a church-yard; thick and sad
    The tombstones stand in melancholy rows;
And 'mid the graves, in sable garments clad,
    Pale Memory walks, still weeping as she goes.

There many a joy hath found an early tomb,
    Departed hopes that once were bright and young,
Loves that were blasted in their tender bloom,
    Sweet friendships poisoned by the slanderer's tongue.

Yea, they are gone; those joys are dead and sere;
    Those cherished hopes and loves have passed away;
Some have been wept for many a weary year,
    And some were buried only yesterday.

There is a Resurrection from the tomb,
    Its sleeping sons shall start to life again;
But when, O Heart, shall thy Revival come,
    And all thy dead awake? Oh, When? Ah, When?

The heart is like a church-yard: thick and sad
    The tombstones stand in melancholy rows;
And 'mid its graves, in solemn mourning clad,
    Pale Memory walks, still weeping as she goes.

M. A. COURTNEY.

The White Ladie.

Now, fifty years ago, may be,
   On a wild winter's night,
To the ceaseless moaning of the sea,
This legend of the " White Ladie,"
   Was told by firelight.

She was a proud and haughty dame
   Of old Penkivell's race ;
He had no son to bear his name ;
He worshipped her, and who could blame,
   In the old Squire's place ?

Though centuries have passed away,
   Her home may still be seen,—
A granite building, low and grey,
Storm-beaten, often flecked with spray,
   In the parish of Pendeen.

Her name was Avis ; there were few
   In Cornwall fair as she,
Her eyes were a deep hyacinth blue,
Her cheeks had the pink creamy hue
   We in the wild rose see.

Her hair was red, with gleams of gold,
   And rippled round her head ;
But she was false,—her heart was cold ;
Her soul for money she'd have sold ;
   Pride was her daily bread.

From all the parishes around
   Brave suitors came to woo ;
But in her sight none favour found,
She cared more for her horse and hound
   Than loyal hearts and true.

Would only no denial take
   Her uncle Uther's son ;
He thought of her asleep, awake ;
He courted dangers for her sake,
   And vowed she should be won.

For her he'd often crossed the sea
   In search of laces rare,
Brocades and silks, that she might be
Decked out in all her bravery,
   The fairest of the fair.

For Cornishmen, in days of yore,
   Thought smuggling was no crime ;
And John Lenine, who knew the shore,
Had brought from France, like many more,
   Rich ventures in his time.

A secret subterranean way
   Ran 'twixt her house and beach ;
Through a dark cave the entrance lay,
Known to few dwellers in the bay,—
   Most difficult to reach.

But dangers never daunted John;
   By it one night he brought
Avis, when folks to rest had gone,
Some gauds she'd set her heart upon;
   To win her thus he thought.

She took his gifts, but mocked his woe:
   Said, "Cousin, this I'll do,
When summer comes with frost and snow,
Or roses in mid-winter blow,
   Why then—I'll marry you!

"I swear I will. Next Christmas-day
   A red rose to me bring,
My answer then shall not be nay,
And as a pledge for what I say,
   You may—give me a ring."

In a few days the ring was sent,
   And then John sail'd afar;
In quest of the red rose he went;
To wed her still his soul was bent;
   Hope was his guiding star.

He had been gone three months or more;
   Christmas was drawing nigh;
Slipped in, and anchored close to shore,
A man-of-war, that once before,
   In Pendeen Bay did lie.

Of her were many stories told,—
   How, under shade of night,
She'd sent forth men, like wolves on fold,
Who'd carried off the young and old,
   For James, the King, to fight.

This dreadful ship returned again,
   Made many women sad:
Some feared to lose their boys: with pain
Some wept for husbands "pressed" and slain;
   Avis alone was glad.

She knew the captain,—thought that he
  Could wealth and rank bestow ;
For them he might her husband be,
For never wed a man would she
  Who could no rent-roll show.

He was not there to woo a bride,
  For men alone he came ;
But still he flattered, fed her pride,
With honeyed words and gifts he plied
  This most imperious dame.

Because through her he wished to learn
  The secret hidden way,
From whence it ran, where made a turn,
When John was likely to return,
  And why he'd gone away ?

The traitress told him all—The vow
  She'd pledged herself to keep ;
Said John at home would soon be now ;
Wished he would "press him," cared not how ;
  If killed, she should not weep.

Meanwhile poor John, who'd sailed away,
  The bright, red rose to find,
Had heard in Nice a sailor say
" That roses bloomed on Christmas-day,"
  And Fate to him was kind.

For, walking down a crooked street,
  There in a house he spied
A rose-tree bearing blossoms sweet ;
He entered in with eager feet,
  Nor long did there abide

Before 'twas his. Full many a crown
  For that rose-bush he paid.
Quick to his ship he bore it down,
Again set sail for Penzance town,
  And a prosperous voyage made.

His tree he guarded with great care,
   But the flowers faded fast;
Its branches soon were nearly bare
Of all its blossoms late so fair,—
   One rose remained—the last.

He reached his home on Christmas-day
   As the joy-bells out did ring;
Red rose in hand, he went his way
To meet his cousin, blithe and gay;
   His heart did carols sing.

He bent his steps towards the shore
   The hidden path to take,
But ere he reached the secret door,
Set on him ten stout men or more,
   A captive him to make.

He fought for life, whilst holding still
   The red rose in his hand;
And many of his foes did kill,—
Was wounded oft, yet fought on, till
   Lay stretched upon the sand

He and the Captain side by side,
   Both bleeding unto death.
The treachery of his would-be bride
John heard,— spake not a word, and died;
   But with his dying breath

The Captain cursed her; bade a lad
   The rose to Avis bear,
Wet with his blood: "Tell her she had
Her wicked wish, might now be glad,
   And it in triumph wear."

She lived till she was very old,
   But never from that day
The sun shone on her; she was cold
In hottest June, for she had sold,
   And sworn a life away.

No shadow from her body cast
   E'er played upon the ground.
Shunned by all men, she lived alone,
And when death claimed her for his own,
   Her soul no respite found.

Each Christmas morn she doth appear,
   At the entrance o' the cave,
Holding her rose. She striketh fear :
Who sees her knows the coming year
   Will find him in his grave.

Three Days.

FIRST DAY.

LIFE for me is full of gladness !
   One long holiday.
Other people talk of sadness ;
   I am always gay.
Songs to my lips unbidden spring ;
I sing because I needs must sing.

Like as the birds, who, winter past,
   Pour from bush and tree,
Forgetting its keen chilling blast,
   Sweetest melody.
Blackbirds and thrushes all day sing ;
Flowers and love come with the Spring.

'Tis Spring with me ; the love have I
   Of a good man and true ;
The paths of life I tread now lie
   Through roses, fresh with dew ;
Blithe in my ears the old tune rings,—
A happy heart it always sings.

But why should I not happy be
  When I am grey and old ?
Flowers may fade, youth pass away,
  But love can ne'er grow cold.
No, only death should sorrow bring ;
Till that comes, heart, cease not to sing.

NEXT YEAR.

A twelvemonth since and I was gay ;
  Now I am sad.
For my lost joys I weep alway,—
  Cannot be glad.
My songs are hushed ; the roses dead ;
Spring gone ; the singing birds have fled.

I thought that death alone could part
  Those that were true.
That I should bear an aching heart
  I little knew.
But idle words were lightly said,
And all my hopes lay withered,—dead.

Since then for my dear love in vain
  I've pined. It seems
I may not see his face again
  Except in dreams.
Each night I long to make my bed
Where lie in heaps the brown leaves dead.

A month ago, in bitter scorn,
  Will went from me ;
A neighbour told me yester morn
  He'd gone to sea.
My love yet lives. Can his be dead ?
It may be bruised—not withered.

MANY YEARS AFTER.

I sat beside my fire, lived o'er again
My happy youth, now left so far behind ;
Outside I heard the splash of heavy rain,
The ceaseless soughing of the stormy wind,

The melancholy moaning of the sea,
The rush of great waves, breaking on the shore;
When suddenly a loved voice called on me,
A much loved voice I thought to hear no more.

I caught my breath and listened. Softly fell,
In pleading tones, my name upon mine ear;
Then, like a sigh, was breathed the word "Farewell;"
My sad heart failed me, my limbs shook with fear.

I hurried to the shore,—there, still afloat,
A noble vessel 'mongst the breakers lay;
Our men were trying to push off their boat;
We women could do nought but watch and pray.

Three times the lifeboat launched. Alas, in vain!
All hands were lost! The ship became a wreck.
The face of one drowned man I saw again—
He wore my miniature around his neck!

THE "HARRIS" FAMILY.

JOHN HARRIS.

Selected verses from

An Ode

*On the Tercentenary Anniversary of William Shakespere,
April 23rd, 1864.*

PRIZE POEM.

Over the earth a glow,
Peak-point and plain below,
The red round sun sinks in the purple west;
Lambs press their daisy bed,
The lark drops overhead,
And sings the labourer, hastening home to rest.

Bathed in the ruddy light,
Flooding his native height,
A youthful bard is stretched upon the moss;
He heedeth not the eve
Whose locks the elfins weave,
Entranced with Shakespere near a Cornish cross.

Men pass him and repass;
The hare is in the grass;
The full moon stealeth o'er the hill of pines;
Twilight is lingering dim;
The village vesper hymn
Murmurs its music through the trembling vines.

* * * * *

A spell is on his soul:
He scans the mystic scroll
Of human passions wakened by the wand
Of England's noblest seer,
Whom England holds so dear,—
Great, glorious Shakespere, loved in every land!

* * * * *

He solved the human heart
Like mariner his chart,
And Passion's every phase was known to him;
And when the full time came,
Forth burst the mighty flame,
To blaze and brighten till the stars are dim.

* * * * *

And so, great bard, to-day
We weave thy natal lay,
And cluster gratefully around thy name:
England will ever be,
Dear Shakespere, proud of thee,
And coming ages but augment thy fame.

My Last Lay.

(The last poem published in " Last Lays," the 17th and last volume of John Harris's poems.)

I STAND like one upon a reach of elms,
By the Great River's shore—
Listening for voices from untrodden realms,
Which thrill me evermore.

My staff is lying by a mound of flowers,
  My weary feet at rest,
And echoes haunt me in song-ringing showers
  From regions of the blest.

A mystic Hand comes through the fading light,
  Which I but dimly see,
And takes my lyre, and bears it out of sight,—
  The Hand that gave it me.

The sky-taught bird, and lesser shining shapes
  That in the hedgerows dwell,
Or gather to the concert of the capes,
  Breathe forth their sad farewell.

My Last Lay holds a benediction bright
  For friends and patrons kind,
Who filled my hemisphere with purer light,
  Which leaves a glow behind.

Selection from

"Monro."

(A Biographic Sketch of the Poet's life.)

And when the pulse of life shall throb no more
  At His command, and its red currents freeze,
When silence comes, and busy day is o'er,
  Monro would sleep beneath her whispering trees,
Where sing the birds, and hum the homeward bees,
  And blush the flowers when Spring is passing by,
As notes unnumbered float upon the breeze,
  And he will watch her from the upper sky,
And at eve's musing hour will sometimes near her fly.

Farewell! Farewell! A voice is in his ear,
   That Time's fleet hour-glass is expending fast,
The glittering grains run faster year by year,
   With soundless drop, and soon will fall the last.
O Thou, who through the gloomy grave hast past,
   Send Thy good Spirit to renew our own !
May doubt and fear for ever be outcast,
   And then uplift us to Thy glorious throne,
Where faith expands no more, and perfect love is known !

His task is ended, and he feels like one
   Whose boat is rocking 'neath the island trees,
Where gorgeous birds are fluttering in the sun,
   And harps ring sweetness on the sauntering breeze.
The hills and vales, where hum the honey bees,
   Are those he laboured to discover long,
Sailing, hope-beckoned, over unknown seas,
Though fierce winds blew, and beat the billows strong.
Once more farewell ! farewell ! Thus closeth Monro's song.

J. HOWARD HARRIS.
A Cornish Welcome.
(Inscribed to F. C.)

A WANDERER comes in summer time,
   From distant London's din,
To visit haunts of boyhood days,—
   The " Land of Fish and Tin."
We'll tune for him a homely lay
And wish him health for many a day.

The sea, the sky, the home-bound boat,
   The ocean's solemn roar,
Bring fancies dear of other days :
   He loves them more and more.
Thus in our path from youth to age
There's many a line on Memory's page.

The " hueva's " cry, the " seiner's " shout,
    Ring in his ears to-day,
While glittering sunlight tips the waves
    Of ever-dear Mount's Bay.
Far from these scenes his steps may roam,
But loving still are thoughts of home.

Time's chariot wheels turn round and round
    With load of joy or pain;
The winter o'er,—the summer come,—
    We'll welcome him again.
May Cornish hearts and hands be true,
And friendship's faith be ever new.

Woven Fancies.

The gossamers swing in the summer light
    From leaflets all covered with dew;
The pearl drops gleam with their fairy spells
    In crimson and golden hue.

The threads fly fast in the fact'ry high,
    Weaving the fabric rare,
To gladden the cottager's sunburnt child,
    Or brighten the lady fair.

The whirring wheels whirl round and round,
    As in the rope-walk low
The hempen strands weave mighty bands,
    While the spinners backward go.

So love weaves sure from day to day
    A sweet and shadowy chain;
Its gossamer links are small and thin
    For bearing the world's cold strain.

Though light as air that woven chain
    Each thread is tried and true;
Old Time is strength'ning the tiny cords,
    And drawing my love to you.

JOHN ALFRED HARRIS.

Lay of the Bereaved.

And art thou gone from us, my father dear,
    And is thy gentle, loving spirit fled ?
O ! thou in life we loved so well
    Art resting in thy lowly, silent bed !
And never shall we hear again
    Thy welcomed tread.

Thy chair is vacant by our lonely hearth ;
    Thy staff's at rest behind the study door ;
Thy quill and ink are on the mantel-shelf ;
    But now thine earthly lays are o'er.
For thou art gone with saints to sing
    On Zion's golden shore.

My pen grows feeble, father mine,
    Thy quiet, cheering deeds to write :
To tell of all thy lasting, loving worth ;
    But thine example bright
Shall cheer us daily on life's pilgrim road,
    And guide our steps aright.

The world, perchance, will miss thee not,
    Nor heed thy simple minstrel lays ;
But He who knows the smallest sparrow's fall
    Did heed thine unobtrusive ways :
Well pleased His child should sow the precious seed,
    And scatter Gospel rays.

Thy pen at all times thou didst wield
    In cause of Truth and Right,
Instead of lauding feats of wrong
    And warlike deeds of might :
But for the sinner sighed and prayed
    And led to Calvary's Height.

Hushed is thy lyre, its cords are mute ;
    But still we feel thee nigh,
Though days are dark and drear to us,—
    My mother dear and I.
O Father ! take our hands and onward lead
    To be with thee on high.

Farewell ! Farewell ! and once again farewell !
    My gentle, gifted, loving sire !
Safe in that heavenly city bright,
    Among the white-robed choir,
Thy songs are raised to Christ alone,
    From off thy golden lyre.

RICHARD HAMBLY.

Our Sand-hills.

[Church Tradition.]

WE love our Cornish land—
For aught its hills of sand,
Mines unromantic, and its stormy coasts—
For in the barren mound
Are richer memories found,
Than many a ruin of famed castle boasts.

No gilded mausoleum,
Or strains of rich Te Deum,
Allure the traveller where these heroes lie;
In life, by precept holy,
They sought the poor and lowly,
And hoped in death no tribute 'neath the sky.

Honour those men of old,
Whose faith and courage bold,
In the first ardour of the church's youth,
Transplanted to our shores,
Far richer than its ores,
The quenchless fibres of a heaven-born Truth!

'Tis said from Erin's Isle—
   Ere war, and priestly guile,
Had dulled the brightness of its emerald green—
   They crossed in open boat,
   And made the cheery note
Lighten the horrors of the voyage between.

   They found our altars red
   With blood of human dead,
From the crushed victims of an iron spell;
   They told of Him who died—
   And soon at eventide
Was heard the music of the church-going bell.

   And still these churches stand,
   Part hidden in the sand
Raised by the fury of Atlanta's wave;
   And there these heroes sleep—
   Come, let us reverent seek,
Nor heedless trample on, their honoured graves.

Mount's Bay.

How fine the out-look on a summer's day,
From open window near thy shores, Penzance!
Or seated on thy well-kept promenade,
The eyes set free from page of old romance,
To gaze far out upon the sea and sky.
Now, turn delighted to yon noble Mount—
Home of St. Aubyn, crowned with costly pile—
To which tradition, with its gilded pen,
Gives angel visit, hence St. Michael named:
More veritable fact and glorious still,
Trod by Victoria, our gracious Queen.
Nor wearied yet, trace out those farther shores,
Where hides Porthleven, 'neath the bluff headland,
Its busy trade, its ships and pleasant walks;
And onward still, nigh lost in purple haze,
See the tall cliffs of far-famed Lizard rise!

These on the left: to right, with less expanse,
The verdurous slopes of Paul and Mousehole stretch,
With Newlyn nestled in the seaward curve;
Homes of the fishermen, whose gallant craft
Dot the blue waters of the tranquil bay.
These are thy glories, Town and Bay and Mount—
Sketched with but hasty and deficient hand—
That bring the tourist to thy pleasant homes,
To fish, to bathe, to roam along thy coasts:
These breathe new life into the jaded mind,
And charm the feverish into rest and peace.

What the Round Shell says.

I PICKED up a shell, which the ocean
   Had dropped on the sounding shore,
And bore it away to the inland,
   A hundred good miles or more.

And long it has lain on the mantel—
   Away from the sounding shore,
Away from the scream of the sea-bird,
   Away from the ocean's roar—

Yet whenever I stoop to listen
   To what the round shell will say,
There comes from its heart a low murmur,
   As of waves breaking far away;

A murmur of billows and seaweed,
   Of wind thro' the ocean caves,
Of laughter and voices—which mem'ry
   Calls back from their far-off graves.

And oft, now I'm sick and weary,
   And life is sure passing away,
I take the round shell from the mantel,
   To catch what it still would say;

For my heart seems to join in its echo,
   And to lie, as a shell, on life's shore,
From which the blue waters are ebbing,
   To return and wrap round me no more.

And I'm waiting till one of God's angels,
   Who visit this sea-girt strand,
Shall take me — a shell of life's ocean —
   To a place in the Better Land.

Music.

Methinks the noblest form of song
   Is music of the mind,
Which only thought can formulate,
   And waken'd fancy find.

Such music as the poet feels,
   When deep in mystic scroll,
He enters, with a noiseless step,
   The temple of the soul;

And hears, along its shadowy aisles,
   The secret whisper creep,
And melodies, of wondrous power,
   Among its arches sweep.

Scarce less is he who music hears
   In nature everywhere,
A solo in the running brook,
   And concerts in the air;

Rich movements in the waving pines,
   Mixed voices in the deep —
Now raging as in angry mood,
   Now gentle as in sleep.

But men are few whose souls are moved
   By nature's myriad strains,
Which thunder from her mountain tops,
   And murmur o'er her plains;

And fewer still who, seeking, find
   The springs of human thought,
And enter on the poet's land,
   Where music comes unsought.

Still, to rejoice the hearts of men
   'Mid earth's engrossing care,
God, in the garden of each soul,
   Hath placed this seedling rare,

This inborn sense of harmony—
   Which rising through the soul,
Can fill each part with melody,
   And happiness the whole.

And he who, glad acknowledging
   Its high and heavenly birth,
Shall set to themes ennobling
   Its music here on earth;

Shall, when a general death has hushed
   All harmony below,
With soul attuned to nobler strains
   On high for ever glow.

"The Next Thing."

Not what inclination
Or fashion would suggest,
   Not that situation
More lofty than the rest,
Not the goal that's nearest,
Not the path that's clearest,
   But the *next* thing.
Not where skies are bluest,
And the storms are fewest,
Not the word that easeth,
Not the task that pleaseth,
   But the *next* thing.

That which duty prompteth,
That which love suggests,
That which makes thee happier
  In thyself and guests.
The word that is the truest,
  The song that is the best,
The pathway that is purest,
  More useful than the rest;
The place that e'en if dying,
  Thou would'st not fear to be;
The work that most is needed
  For God, the world and thee.

"God Bless You."

A FAITH, a prayer, it cometh oft
From aged lips, while on the soft,
Waved hair of youth, that rev'rent stands,
  Are placed the hands.

Love's fervent wish, it falleth warm
From trembling lips — true Christian charm!
Uttered when near, if distant, then
  By speech of pen.

It glistens bright on history's scroll,
A phrase of light! making the soul
Of the far past give utterance true,
  Heathen and Jew.

Not obsolete! It floweth still
From life's full spring — perennial rill,
That murmurs soft where'er we plod,
  Of love and God.

Love.

Love is the ocean, when it swells
    And flows upon the land,
Caressing with its waves and shells
    The dull forsaken strand.

Love is the carol of the bird,
    The light of summer's sun,
The calm of twilight softly stirred
    By symphonies of home.

Love is the sweetest scent of flower,
    The ripest taste of fruit,
The soft-descending vernal shower,
    That laves the tender shoot.

Love is the brightly glistening tear
    Of heart that, joyous, weeps;
An angel-form, that hovers near
    Where childhood dreams and sleeps.

Love is the firmament of blue,
    The stars on stillest night,
The blessed name of God most true—
    Author of Love and Light.

"I'm Tired."

So lisps the child, whose tiny feet
Have pattered long o'er mazy street,
Or country lane; as now it rests,
    With crumpled cap,
    On nurse's lap.

So yawns the worker, as the round
Of arduous tasks, at length has found
A welcome end; and sitting now
    To think or read,
    Makes little speed!

Thus murmurs age, whose lengthened race
Is well-nigh run, and soon a place
Will lose on earth—but not in heaven !
    So will we pray
    For hair of grey.

Thus sighs the suff"rer, as the night
Drags weary on ; yet hope turns bright
To that Far Land, where none are sick,
    Nor ever say,
    " Ah ! weary day.'

LINA HOWELL.

Canzonet.

"Marguerite! Marguerite!" call the lilies
    Across the dewy lawn,—
"Come with thy smile to welcome
  The flush of laughing Dawn.

"Come, we are weary waiting;
    Already Dawn has passed,
And o'er our sleeping petals
  A flood of dewdrops cast.

"We were dreaming when she woke us,
    As she cried—'Awake! 'tis day!'
And we heard her call the song-birds
  As she passed along her way.

"Marguerite! Marguerite!" call the roses,
    "Come, with thy face so fair,—
Come with the golden sunrays,
  Agleaming on thy hair.

The clematis bells are ringing
　　Beneath the sheltered eaves,—
" Come, with thine eyes like violets,
　　Dew-steeped beneath their leaves.

" Come, with thy fairy footsteps,—
　　O'er the modest daisies trip ;
Come, with thy sweet face blushing,
　　Tinged like each daisy lip."

" Marguerite ! Marguerite ! " calls the streamlet,
　　As it runs towards the sea,
" In the mirror of my shining depths
　　The Nereides wait for thee."

The song-birds sing " She is coming
　　Over the meadow way ;
We can hear her fresh voice singing
　　Some chanson bright and gay."

" We can see her," sing the roses,—
　　" Her head with its sunny sheen ; "
And one tall lily murmurs
　　" She is coming—My queen, my queen ! "

Told by the Bells.

Up to my window floating, from the busy city street,
I hear the hum of voices and the tread of many feet—
Fresh young children's voices, and footsteps bright and glad,
Voices worn by sorrow, and footsteps slow and sad—
Faces sweet and gentle, and faces lined with care,
Gleaming golden tresses, and locks of silvery hair.
What message do ye bring, oh, bells, across the snow,
To this poor tide of human life, so rapid in its flow ?
Perchance in many hearts ye stir old memories once again ;
Perchance to many eyes ye bring swift tears of silent pain ;

Perchance some hearts are dead to heed the story in thy
    chimes—
The story angel voices told back in the olden times,
When, bending o'er the snow-clad hills, their radiant wings
    unfurled,
And they sung their heavenly carol above a sleeping world.

To-day 'tis the same old story the angels told of then,
Bringing the same old message to the changing hearts of
    men :
Striking again the same old chord upon the harp of life,
Until its ringing echoes float above all earthly strife.
Oh, bells, ye bring me a picture, as if the unseen hand
Of some strange and mystic artist had strayed from the
    Spirit Land,
And painted in darkened shadows a garret cold and bare.
Surely ye cannot bring a dream of gladness there,
Where the cold pale light of a candle its ghostly glimmers
    shed
Upon a worn and pallid face and o'er a drooping head ;
And slowly fall the blinding tears upon her dreary work,
The ceaseless stitch and endless toil she knows she dare not
    shirk.

Peace to that weary heart !—oh, bells, it cannot be—
And her tired lips gave answer—" There is no peace for me.
My only guest is Want—'tis Want that grimly stands,
Guarding my lonely threshold, and pointing, with bony
    hands,
To my hearth, where no embers flicker and no cheery fire-
    light falls
With warm and friendly greeting upon the cold blank walls.
Why do ye come to taunt me, oh, bells, with your dreams of
    peace ?
Would I might still your echoes and bid your voices cease.
Yet once I loved your music— before the dazzling gleams
Of the city's light fell on me, and broke my childish dreams.
Those dreams and vanished faces—oh, bells, ye rouse them
    now,
Their memories hang like fetters around my aching brow,"

" List to the King's own message, His promise shall not fail ;
Be still, poor tired heart, there's peace behind the veil."

The picture has changed ; and another, as bright as that
    was sad,
Shines on me through the shadows : there all is gay and glad.
Gathered around the hearth where the ruddy firelight glows,
And o'er bright merry faces its dancing flamelight throws ;
Falling across the dim old room, and o'er each childish head,
Lighting up beneath their leaves the berries white and red—
I hear their joyful voices in some ballad quaint and sweet,
And their merry-hearted laughter and little dancing feet ;
Surely ye bring, oh, bells, a peaceful message there ?
Ah, yes, but on that hearth there stands a vacant chair.

When yester year we chimed, another little voice
Echoed across the threshold, and bade all hearts rejoice.
On the hearth a little form lingered to watch the bright logs
    roar,
And the music of other footsteps echoed across the floor.
A little face watched at the window the feathery snowflakes
    fall ;
A little hand wreathed the berries upon the old oak wall.
Only a speaking silence sits in her vacant chair ;
Only the snow-drifts cover her crown of golden hair.
Yet close again to the threshold, with angel wings of light,
Her unseen presence lingers upon that hearth to-night.
"The broken links on earth "—they hear her softly sing—
"Shall be bound again in Heaven, is the message of the King."

Tokens.

    Only some scentless blossoms,
        Once sweet and passing fair,
    Only a few old letters,
        Bound with a tress of hair ;
    Only a knot of ribbon
        And a glove half torn in two,
    Only a satin slipper
        And a ring of turquoise blue.

Only some rusty needles,
   And silken thread flung by,
Only a palette laden
   With colours hard and dry ;
Only a picture lying
   Half finished in the shade,
Only a jewelled hand-screen,
   Upon the table laid.

Only a book with pages
   Turned down just here and there,
Only a " Strad " with broken strings
   Upon a favourite chair ;
Only a bowl of rose leaves,
   In the dusk of the silent room,
Only a song once echoed
   In the hush of the twilight gloom.

Only a moon-lit garden,
   With rows of lily sheaves,
Only instead of footsteps
   The sigh of falling leaves ;
Only a window opened
   To the balmy evening air,
Only a wistful yearning
   For a face no longer there.

Miserere Domine.

It stood without a convent gate, an old cross worn and grey,
And 'neath it, sobbing in the mist, the wild sea rolled away ;
Across the weather-beaten stone sweet passion flowers clung,
And 'round the letters quaintly carved their clinging tendrils hung.
Years had come and years had gone, yet still the children play'd
With laughing lips and sunny eyes beneath the convent's shade ;
And when the vesper chimes rang out upon the balmy air,
With solemn eyes and voices hushed they breathed the cross's prayer,   Miserere Domine.

As each life holds its story, so the old cross held its own,
A story known to the flowers and the restless waves alone ;
Some strange romantic halo still linked it to the past,
And ghosts of unforgotten years their shadows o'er it cast.
There many a tired wanderer would rest beside the way,
Where hot and fierce the noonday sun across the landscape lay,
Old men with careworn faces and silvery sprinkled hair
In faltering tones gave echo to the cross's silent prayer,
     Miserere Domine.

The soft winds crept across it in the fleeting summer hours,
And the gleams of sunset lingered amid the passion flowers ;
There life within the high stone walls was perfect in its rest,
A tranquil stream with heaven's light upon its quiet breast.
Oft-times some sad-eyed girl recluse, alone with sea and sky,
Would linger there to whisper to the world a last good-bye,
Ere the convent gate behind her closed, and rang her parting
 knell,
In the wailing chant that followed the Ave the old prayer
 rose and fell,
     Miserere Domine.

She came when the shadows were falling adown the convent
 wall,
And o'er the mountains floated the tinkling sheep bells' call.
Her feet were worn and weary, and her eyes were dim with
 tears,
As she gazed upon her old home, her home of bye-gone years,
When her dauntless soul had hungered and yearned for
 light afar,
And fled away like a captive bird freed from its prison bar.
She'd left the path behind her to tread the path before,
Though angel hands had held her back and breathed the
 prayer of yore,
     Miserere Domine.

With ruthless hands she'd scattered the lilies of her youth,
To gather Pleasure's roses before the blooms of Truth ;
She'd trod a flowery pathway in one brief golden morn,
Yet knew not 'neath each blossom there lurked a cruel thorn ;
Her hollow eyes and thin wan face all told a tale of woe,

And her childlike trust had vanished like her rich warm
    southern glow.
Adown the hillside falling, a darker shadow swept,
And a crown of glory glistened where the passion flowers
    slept;
But lo! the flowers faded, and a tender face instead
Shone out with eyes of pity beneath a thorn-crowned head.
At the foot of the cross, in shadow, a wild white face had
    grown,
The face of a miserable sinner, and she knew it for her own,
She knew it, and in her dreaming the past was swept away,
Behind her lay the darkness and before a shining way,—
'Twas only the moonbeams flooding the sea with a mystic
    glow,
While the lips of the dreamer murmured in broken tones and
    low,
                                  Miserere Domine.

J. DRYDEN HOSKEN.

Selections from

"Phaon and Sappho,"
and short Poems.

[Included by kind permission of Messrs Macmillan and Co., and the Author, who hold the Copyright.]

"Phaon and Sappho" is a Greek Drama, the scene of which is laid in Mytylene, in Lesbos.

A confession of love:—

Phaon. Sweet excellence, scorn not at Nature's tongue;
The deepest chords within me you have stirred;
As though the wing of some air-travelling God
Had touched the strings of some disused lyre;
As I an instantaneous change do feel,
And my old nature turns away from me,
So will I tie description of my state
In one sweet word, list! —*love!*

Phaon vows constancy:—

I will attend on you
As constant as the shadow of the world
Thrown on the orb-paved heaven.

And Sappho says :—

          O Phaon, we must part.
The day hath spent its fury out, and light
Dies slowly upward from the valley's depths
Along the mountain side, until its peak
Retains the last gold spark of hurrying day,
Flung like a fair memorial of his love
Back to the grieving earth ; but he will rise
And with him our new life of happiness.

       *   *   *   *   *

Phaon. Now, Brassidas, comes on my flood of joy ;
I hold this breath while thinking of my love,
Lest the keen sense of pleasure strike me dead.
O ! that I were as rich as my desire,
That I might coin the very horn of fortune
Into some sign of wealth, to shew my Love
The manifested estimation
In which I hold her worth : but could that do it ?
No ! nor all earth beside—I am a fool
From sheer excess of joy.

       *   *   *   *   *

Sappho. Rest there, fair Goblet. O ! my joy in death,
Not all the winds of heaven lend thee one breath
To speak one word in Sappho's hungry ear,—
No life for thee, tho' life for all beside !
And still a smile upon those lips of thine—
O ! mockery of life !—I read the thought
That fluttered from thee with thy last drawn breath,
And hangs even now on heaven. O ! Phaon ! Phaon !
To meet like this ! that this should be the end,
Of Love's fair promise ! O ! my breathless love !
Can I not coax thee back to life again ?
List ! 'tis thy Sappho speaking unto thee—
O foolish grief !—come resolution—come !
Give me strength to enact my dreaded part :—

All other thought be gone!—within this Goblet
There is a poison death doth smile to own.
I am a priestess still unto Revenge,
And here I pour libations to that Power,
And now do give myself a sacrifice
To appease the Manes of my lover dead
Whose death I helped apace. (*Drinks from Goblet*).
                                          Now do I sleep
To waken by my love. (*Dies*).

Song.

Sink gently in the silent sea,
   Die slowly, slowly in the west;
Lull'd by the winds sweet minstrelsy
   To golden rest.

Thy wak'ning I shall view no more
   Behind the east's pale shimmering hills;
Ere thou dost rise the tale is o'er
   Of earthly ills.

Destiny.

Where heaven, bright flashing thro' the deeps
   Of this enduring universe,
Gleams brilliant with its massy steeps,
   There sits a power to man averse,
Which ever hurls him to and fro,
Bound with its chains where'er he go.

'Tis Destiny, that through our life
   To tempt us, drops its golden ball.
When we are anxious in the strife
   That should secure for us our all,
Comes Destiny to thwart our aim,
And leave us nothing but a name.

Fell power! at war for aye with man,
  Why hauntest thou his game of chance?—
Himself a strange imperfect plan,
  His life a bauble. Cast thy glance
And shake thy awful brow again,
Thou can'st not add another pain.

A Day in Spring.

Hail! season of delight and song,
Once more you tint the glowing skies,
And wake the busy insect throng
While strewing earth with thousand dyes:
The primrose and anemones,
The daisy prim and violet blue
In clustering colonies arise
Where'er I turn my raptured view,
Still speaking to the heart of things for ever new.

And now the sun is high o'erhead,
The noontide silence reigns around,
The floweret droops its weary head,
And echo listens for a sound.
Now far away I catch the bound
Of sea-waves, and the distant splash
Within the forest shades has found
An answering voice, the whirring dash
Of startled bird resounds from yonder moss-grown ash.

Here I, at large, could moralize
Upon the mis-spent life of man,
Comparing him to that which lies
For our good heed thro' Nature's plan.
But lo! an end to day's bright span,
The sun is drooping in the main,
The evening breeze begins to fan
The sleeping woods, while his last strain
The song-bird pours away upon the dark'ning plain.

O ! Spring-time, passing fast away,
Would I could live with thee for ever,
Where never sorrow, age, decay
The spirit from its joy could sever ;
But thou art passing, passing, never
Again to render up the past,
And hours spent with thee, down Time's river
Remorselessly thy hands have cast—
Will they ne'er live again ? only in memory last ?

The Order of the World.

My heart sinks when I look upon the world
   And see the wronger cased in evil might ;
The bloody flag of hell at large unfurled,
   While vice and misery clothe themselves in night ;
The cry of innocence, the growl of lust,
   Fair claims despised, and unjust avarice,
Merit and honour trampled in the dust,
   While sin and virtue are made casting dice,
Shook in the cup of Custom, held by Time,
   With all humanity to watch the game.
Time was when all injustice, woe and crime
   Were straight redressed by heroes of fair fame.
     O ! that we had those old knights' chivalry,
     The wronged to succour, and the slave to free.

A Memory of Love.

How sweet the transient dream and reverie,
   Like twilight's purple wing, sank on my heart
In that fair season when I sat by Thee
   List'ning thy song that shamed Apollo's art.
Love breathes upon my memory, and I see
   The scene within my mind lost in time past,
The ceaseless sun descending in the sea,

The hugh dark waves against the boulders cast,
The solitude of nature, if such be,
The momentary lull, broke by the roar
Of billows, or the sea-birds' noisy glee
Around the time-sapp'd crags and gully's hoar,
While thou wert by me: still in these I find
A shadow of thy presence left behind.

Love and Earth's Echoes.

1 Lover

Love that is spoken often dies,
Quick as the light in evening skies,
Or as a song upon the year,
And leaves no answering spirit near:
Wilt thou be true? Shall I ne'er rue
My plighted faith? Wilt thou be true?

Echo.
Wilt thou be true?

2 Lover.

That doubt, O! maiden, do not name,—
Changeless as yon eternal flame
My spirit evermore shall be
In its full worshipping of thee.
I will be true! Thou shalt not rue
Thy plighted faith! I will be true!

Echo.
I will be true.

1 Lover.

O! Love, I mourned thy broken faith,
And now I live to mourn thy death,
And, like the echo ringing clear,
Thy voice was false within my ear.
"I will be true." O! echo earth
Are these things only for your mirth?

Echo.
Only for—mirth.

A Lover's Meditation on his Lady.

THE lonely thoughts that issue from my mind,
   Fill this small room with shadows of the world,
Where the unstable state of all mankind
   Before reflection's eye is strangely hurled.
O! foolish man to reckon on a joy,
   Thy trust is founded in uncertainty;
Our hopes do make us fools, a cherished toy
   Shews us but children still—yet but for Thee
This life were valueless. Thou art a gem
   Set on the wrinkled forehead of wide death,
Whose wide diffusive splendour doth condemn
   All thought that undervalues human breath.
     Indebted unto fortune least of all,
       Yet having Thee, still rich, though fortunes thrall.

Genius and Love.

I AM so desolate,
   Genius sighs—
Come, Love, and be my mate,
   Give me thine eyes.

I am aweary,
   Love, give me rest;
Leave me not dreary,
   Give me thy breast.

The lark looks to heaven,
   The flower to the sun;
But my heart is sore riven
   For thy beauty, sweet one.

Give me thy presence,
   My life to enfold;
Then care and sorrow hence,
   My life thou shalt hold.

WILLIAM COCK.

Thoughts from the Birds.

In a smiling field lay a number of birds,
  Their colours were rare to behold;
They struck the eye of the passer-by,
  With their touches of amber and gold.

But among them I noticed some one or two
  Whose colours were ashy and grey;
They struck not the eye of the passer-by—
  They lacked the outside display.

But suddenly up from the ground there arose
  One of the ashy and grey;
It soared in the sky till dazed was the eye,
  And oh! the rich melody!

Its liquid notes rang over them all
  And were wafted far and wide;
The passers-by heard the notes from on high,
  And they thought of nought beside.

And I thought—Ah me!—the world is a field,
  There are men with the outside display ;
But the men who inspire and fill us with fire,
  Are oft-times the ashy and grey.

Failed.

Courage ! my brother ! say not that thou hast " failed ! "
  Thou wilt yet safely reach the farther shore ;
Vainly the tempests hath thy barque assailed,—
  Steer on, brave struggler, 'mid the maddening roar !

Heed not the thunderings of the sullen deep,—
  Fear not the billows that around thee roll ;
Vainly the blinding foam doth o'er thee sweep—
  Held are the forces that would harm thy soul !

Steer thro' the perilous seas ! the day will break,
  Which thou hast looked for long, but looked in vain.
Let not grim doubt supplant thy regal faith ;
  Cast forth thy Truths upon the roaring main.

Oft have I watched thee from the distant shore,
  When nobly thou hast ventured on thy way :
Have heard thy voice above the breakers roar,
  Cheering thy soul with its own melody.

Take heart, my brother ! the world defeats thee now ;
  No sunlit sea awaits such barques as thine ;
'Twas ever thus—but cool thy fevered brow,
  It yet will wake to such a soul as thine !

Lift up thine head, thou child of the Immortal !
  Stern will the voyage be thou hast begun ;
What if thy barque should never reach yon portal ?
  Angels will welcome thee, thou noble son !

Dare then the storm, though high the billows roll,
  Thou wilt yet safely reach the farther shore ;
Tho' all Hell's hosts may terrify thy soul !
  Go forth ! brave struggler, till the conflict's o'er.

Summer.

Awake, my soul! shake off thy shroud of darkness!
    A voice within desires thee awake;
While earth, with her innumerable voices,
    Chants forth her praises at thy golden gate.

Behold the pine trees, waving in the distance!
    The corn-fields smile beneath the ripening sun;
The meadows and the hedges teem with gladness;
    And yet *thy* praises hath not yet begun.

The feathery songsters are alive with music!
    Triumphant notes are warbled all around,
Tuning with joy their offsprings' tender voices,
    In unison with all harmonious sound.

The labourer's voice is one sweet rythmic pæan,
    He goes his round with quick and vigorous tread;
The task is light because the heart is lighter,
    His labour smiles to him of daily bread.

The garden's fragrance fills the breeze with odour,
    The redolence of flowers is grandly thine;
And lovely are the colours, strangely blending,
    Touched with the power of master-hand, Divine!

Awake, my soul! and join the song exultant,—
    Awake! shine forth! dispel the gathered gloom!
Let my glad voice join in the blessed chorus,
    And dreary musings for thy joy make room.

Awake! awake! God's presence fills the heavens,
    The radiant earth, the sunset's sapphire throne!
The supernatural in nature flameth!—
    Symbol sublime of thy eternal home!

The Swan Song.

[JOHN PASCOE, THE TRURO BARD.]

"My throbbing heart! be still! be still!
    And bear thy lot below!
And trust thy God whate'er His will
    To send thee bliss or woe;
The evening shades are gathering round,
    And soon the night will come;
Oh, may my spirit then be found,
    Among the blest at home."

[*Extract from his last Poem.*]

Prophetic lines!—sung by the dying bard,
    Who oft-times charmed us with his potent song;
Whose high immortal outbursts oft-times poured
    A liquid ditty on our feverish tongue.

Still is the Poet now!—he'll sing no more;
    No more shall pang or pain enwrap that brow;
Gathered with singers on the radiant shore,
    Oh! for the song that he could sing us now!

No more shall that poor heart with lonely throb
    Burden his being with unrest and pain,
Or cause a Poet's tears to bathe the sod,
    Like the fierce storm-clouds' tempest-driven rain!

Ascended now, in realms of light and love,
    He's with a royal company, serene and vast;
No longer lonely, for in that haven above
    All singers meet from the eternal past.

No night there! Enrobed, ensphered, he walks
    In light—light from the Eternal throne!
All barriers smashed, far, far, above earth's shocks
    Our Poet dwells—"among the blest at Home."

To Cornubia.

[After reading "Phaon and Sappho," by J. Dryden Hosken.]

AWAKE! O Cornubia! rouse thy slumb'rous frame!
   Tell Albion's sons thou hast a mighty bard!
Make thou a way for his melodious strain,
   Whose song-wrapt soul the mystic muse doth guard.

Wake! O awake! and let thy hills and dales
   Echo the praises that should burst from thee!
Let thy glad voice ring through the silent vales,
   Waking thy sons to his rare melody.

Oh! *one* will yet arise to gild thy name,
   Will weave a garland for thy rugged brow,
Will light thy beacons with a quenchless flame,
   And thy proud form shall 'neath its radiance glow.

Thou shouldst be proud of such a child as this!
   Should hasten now to grasp his proffered hand!
Plant on his noble brow a welcome kiss,
   As thy first-born fit for the classic band.

Wake! then, awake! a glorious hope is thine,
   Peal it afar, and let the world regard;
Soon will it rise, beneath the strains sublime,
   And hasten to applaud Cornubia's bard.

"As Thou Wilt."

"Thy will be done"!
   How hard at times to pray—
Yet prayed the Chosen Son!

When His great heart with lonely anguish throbbed
   In dark Gethsemane,
O'erwhelmed with sorrow 'neath the will of God,
   Yet could that dear voice say—
           "Thy will be done."

My brother, canst thou pray
When wreathed in agony,
  As did this radiant son?

When 'neath the blasts of some destroying storm—
  Some dark Gethsemane,—
Canst thou above it raise thy prostrate form,
  And like thy Master say—
              "Thy will be done?"

Aye, brother, canst thou pray
In thy Gethsemane,
  Like a submissive son?

Oh! safe art thou if thou hast learned that prayer,
  Disaster cannot harm thee nor affright,
Vainly will shriek the minions of despair,
  If, like Him, thou canst say in life's dark night—
              "Thy will be done."

Henry Ward Beecher.

On visiting his old battle-ground, Plymouth Church, Brooklyn.

Oh! thou great Spirit, now enthroned in Light,
  Here may I muse on thee, with throbbing brain—
How o'er the foam-fleck'd waves of Time thy name
  Pealed forth its thunder and its matchless might—
Avenger of the wrong and champion of the right!
  Thou heaven-born warrior, here would I remain
Till my frail Spirit catch thy hallowed flame,
  And revel in the glow of thy God-Light.
Immortal Field! where thou hast nobly trod,
  Freeing the sin-chained slave, mid hostile spears:
Thy quenchless power here thrilled the sin-shook spheres
    And ransomed thousands through thee worshipped God!
      Fade may thy veteran form in yonder grove,
      But in our hearts thy name's embalmed in Love.

In Longfellow's Garden.

Chief of New England's bowers ! to thee I'm drawn
   By some mysterious power that haunts this place ;
Some strange enchantment hangs around this lawn,
     Shedding a mystic glow o'er Nature's face—
        And with a subtle flame
        Kindles the musing brain !
Why should this scene entrance the gazing eye ?
   Where lies the spell that chains me to this grove ?
Why doth the soul leap forth in ecstasy—
   Like a young spirit o'er the fronds of Love ?

Ah ! in these realms a mighty spirit dwelt,
   Who swept with subtle touch a matchless lyre,
Till from its wondrous chords the cold earth felt
     The thrilling music of that ransomed choir
        Who, with melodious voice,
        Once made a world rejoice !
Oh ! thou sweet singer, o'er yon foaming sea
   Thy song oft soothed the old world's wearied brain :
Its mighty heart swelled neath thy minstrelsy :
   In every land was heard thy wondrous strain.
        Till Heaven's serenest ray
        Shone o'er its dark-lit way.
Well might Columbia guard this sacred shrine,
   And keep in fadeless splendour thy dear name ;
Well might her laurels round thy brow entwine,—
   A worthier son ne'er wore the robes of fame.

Chief of New England's bards !—Immortal son !
   Still dost thou breathe in fragrance o'er this place ;
Thy presence still doth haunt this sacred lawn,
     Shedding a mystic light o'er Nature's face—
        And with a subtle flame
        Kindles the musing brain !
Here lies the secret of thy potency,—
   This the strange spell that chains me to this grove ;
And thus the soul leaps forth in ecstasy—
   Like a young spirit o'er the fronds of Love.

In Memoriam.

A. H., BORN, 1863; DIED, 1886.

"DEAD!" Avaunt the thought! *Thou* art not dead!
It is not *death* when the frail form gives way—
So that the struggling spirit might have sway
In its own freedom!
The fleshy barriers that entombed thy spirit
Are for ever shattered!—and now, fit
For the celestial bodies, thou art made
A son of Light and Liberty.
     Let us rejoice!
On the Eternal Shores, with all the good and great
Of all the ages, thou art now encompassed!
     Life's broadest gate
Hath opened on thy vision, and, long ere this,
Thy spirit hath begun the immortal bliss
Of that vast company, who, in light serene,
Develop their great forces. Heaven's brightest sheen
O'ermantles them; empannelled and empalled
By the Great Spirit who them hath called
Into that higher state, thou
Art now the scholar, where discipline and rule
Are unheard-of things: for in that wondrous school
They need no more correction.
While here on earth they felt the rod; but death
Proved their gradation-day, and now, on fuller breadth,
Unhindered by the achings of dull clay,
With them thou flashest in the immortal day
Of Heaven's eternal Light. No night,
No pain, no earth-born gloom
Shall evermore fall on thee; but in the radiant noon
Of that empyreal sphere thou dwellest in peace.

Awhile farewell! We leave thee in thy glory,
And pray that we again shall meet
Within the vale. Ah! when again we meet
Each other, we shall part no more.

W. HERBERT THOMAS.

The Two Wishes.

A ROSE in my garden is nodding its head,
And the sun's crimson glow fills the petals with flame
    As their fragrance is borne on the breeze,
    As aroma floats far on the breeze ;
And breathing the perfume so lavishly shed,
I blush like the rose, but with sorrow and shame,
    At the blots on the book of my Past,
    At the guilt and the ghosts of my Past ;
And I would that the rays which the heavens o'erspread,
Might burn every leaf of the days that are dead.

A lily is swaying above the dark earth,
A stately white flower as pure as snow
    Or the pendulous clouds in the sky,
    The soft fleecy clouds in the sky ;
And my soul is athirst for a holier birth,
For the rapture and peace that the Seraphim know,
    And a heart that is purged of its sin,
    That is free from its passion and sin ;
That is chaste as the lily and stainless as snow,
Yet with Love's crimson roses is warmly aglow.

The Heavenly Messenger.

As the glorified angels were singing a song
    Of rapture and peace in the skies,
God beckoned a cherub from out the glad throng
    And gazed in his innocent eyes.
"Go forth," said the King, "with a message to Earth,
    A message of pity and love;
Be mortal, that souls, through the pangs of thy birth,
    May mount to the star-worlds above."

The harp-strings were swept till the quivering notes
    Burst forth in a pæan of praise
And blended with anthems from millions of throats,
    And the heavens with light were ablaze.
Then the cherub knelt down and was blessed by the King,
    And tenderly bidding adieu
To the choir of seraphs, on wide-spreading wing
    Through the clouds the sweet messenger flew.

My heart was elate with ecstatic delight
    As I held a wee babe to my breast—
A cherub,—the fairest that e'er met my sight,
    Or that loving arms ever caressed.
Like a sunbeam from Heaven, that radiant boy
    Through the windows of Home softly stole,
Dispelling my sorrow and scattering joy
    In the depths of my innermost soul.

Oh God! how I worshipped that beautiful flower—
    That blossom from Paradise blown—
Nor divined that for only a swift-passing hour
    Were its beauty and perfume my own.
My vision saw naught of the cherubic band,
    No harp-notes were borne from the spheres,
Idolatry banished the far spirit-land—
    A baby voice deafened my ears.

I fed on the rippling laughter that broke
   O'er his cheeks like a sparkling wave;
It was ever of him that I lovingly spoke,
   To him every thought fondly gave.
I bent o'er his cradle when Angels of Sleep
   Kissed his eyelids with tremulous breath;
Nor knew that above him would stealthily creep
   The sable-hued Angel of Death.

But a trumpet soon rang in the darkness of night,
   And the cherub was summoned away,
While a torrent of tears fell and blinded my sight,
   And writhing in anguish I lay.
In vain I implored my sweet babe to return
   To my arms and his cradle again;
In vain for his presence my spirit might yearn,
   And my heart feel its horrible pain!

Oh, the deep desolation, the silence and grief!
   How it humbled my pride to the dust!
How I prayed to a merciful God for relief,
   Though the punishment meted was just.
Then the message of peace was revealed to my soul,
   And I knelt at the footstool divine,
And back from the glory I saw the clouds roll,
   And the joy of the pardoned was mine.

When I gaze at the gems that besprinkle the skies
   An angel comes fluttering down,
And tenderly wipes every tear from my eyes
   And shows me his star-jewelled crown.
'Tis my baby, immortal, eternally blest,
   Who comes the glad message to tell—
That when 'neath the turf my frail body shall rest
   My soul with the angels shall dwell.

A Song of Venice.

List! O list, to the sound of the music
    Whispering low to the murmuring sea,
List to the thrill of the quivering harp-strings,
    List to their ravishing melody.
Gaze on the flushes of crimson and purple,
    Watch the red sun as it passes from sight,
See the gay nobles in gliding gondolas,
    Bathed in the softness and beauty of night!

        Stand to your oars, O ye brave gondoliers,
        Silent, that sweetly may fall on our ears
        Music like warbles from nightingales' throats,
        Or echoes of Orpheus' rapturous notes!

Hark! O hark, to the voice of the singer!
    Catch the grand strain that is pealing aloft!
Hark! how it rises!— a prayer to the heavens!—
    List! How it dies away tremblingly soft!
How the dark eyes of the ladies are flashing!
    How the stars burn as the music ascends!
See the lights dance as we flit by the palaces!
    How the rich voice with the throbbing harp blends!

Know ye the charm of the soft Southern starlight?
    Know the delight of Venetian song?
Can ye recall the romance and the beauty
    As in gondolas ye glided along?
Still in my fancy I pass 'neath the arches,
    Still hear the chords from the harp's mellow strings;
Glide once again o'er the blue Adriatic,
    List'ning entranced as the strange minstrel sings!

        Stand to your oars, O ye brave gondoliers,
        Silent, that sweetly may fall on our ears
        Music like warbles from nightingales' throats,
        Or echoes of Orpheus' rapturous notes!

Shadows.

A SONG.

As the twilight shadows gather
   And the earth in slumber lies,
I gaze into memory's mirror
   With eager, longing eyes,
And I see the vanished faces
   Come trooping back again,
And a throb of joy is blended
   With a touch of softened pain.

REFRAIN.

Shadows of gladness, shadows of care,
Visions of beauty wondrously fair,
Glimpses of moments golden and bright,
Shadows of sadness, shadows of night.

From the mist there comes the vision
   Of a little dimpled face,
And my tears fall soft, like dew-drops,
   As the memory I embrace:
I hear the tender echoes
   Of a baby's voice again,
And his breath falls like a zephyr
   As it kisses summer rain.

And now I see in the mirror
   A form I loved too well,
Of a maiden who in spring-time
   Had bound me with a spell.
When the winter winds blew coldly
   She join'd the angel band,
Yet her spirit comes to cheer me
   From the distant shadow-land.

O! the precious twilight shadows
   Of the days of long ago;
We would linger with thy visions,
   But on vapour-clouds they go!

When our soulless dust is wafted
   O'er the earth where now we stand,
Shall we dwell with those who wander
   In the mystic shadow-land?

Battling with Clouds.

Sinks now the sun beyond the distant hill
   As daylight melts and merges into night;
His crimson glory streaming brightly still
   Though gloomy storm-clouds gather for the fight.

How fierce upon the glowing disc they crowd,—
   The sombre legions who would slay his beams,
Yet bursting through the dark and stifling shroud,
   With triumph quivering, shine the conquering beams.

Like Hercules beset with armèd foes,
   The Day-god shoots his streaks of living fire,
Defiant as at dawn when he arose
   And up the sapphire pathway mounted higher.

But now the giant meets his final doom,
   Fresh hosts of night come forth and vengeance claim,
And dying Sol, enwrapped in hideous gloom,
   Sinks lifeless as he breathes one lurid flame.

So struggles man when clouds of Sin and Doubt
   His mind assail and blot his life's fair page,—
The warring legions faced and put to rout,
   Another enemy his waning powers engage:

That foe is Death, who rides a ghostly horse,
   And breathes his deadly vapours on mankind
Till each frail mortal is a silent corse
   And wreaths of tears the victor's forehead bind.

But Sol with undimm'd splendour will arise,
   His golden brightness once more we shall see;
So man shall rise and wear in yonder skies
   A crown of light and immortality!

The Goddess of Fashion.

Great Goddess! In thy courts I fearless stand,
And face a tyrant ruling every land;
In thee behold a despot whose dark sway
Moulds human lives as potters mould their clay.
No monarch seated on his regal throne
Dare give thee battle, or thy claims disown;
More potent than barbaric rulers, thou,
Feared more than Western King with crownèd brow;
Served by the savage and the civilized—
Thy sentence dreaded, and thy favour prized!

Foul deity! Thy cheeks should burn with shame,
Thy glory perish by consuming flame!
The tyrant Nero's hands were steeped in crime,
But thou shedd'st human blood in every clime;
Inflictest torture, exquisitely keen,
And forgest chains for peasant, lord and queen.
At thy command the mother slays her child;
For thee God's sacred image is defiled—
The body mutilated, and the soul
Severed from hope of its eternal goal!

Accursed Goddess! Lo, thy subjects kneel
And kiss thy feet, and for thy smile appeal.
There bends the Indian, with his flatten'd brow,
And there wasp-waisted English matrons bow:
And Chinese dame with " golden lily foot,"
On which Deformity her stamp has put.
The proud Maori chief, with tattoed face,
And South Sea cannibal, have found a place;
Yet still the hosts of slaves and martyrs come,
Who at thy word would be maim'd, deaf and dumb!

How varied, and how hideous, is thy train
Of willing sufferers of horrid pain!
Blinded by Folly, and by Custom bound;
By fear and envy swayed and hemmed around!
Here the Ascetic shows his lengthened nails

To Turkish ladies wrapped in muffling veils;
There the stern Judge struts forth with wig and gown,
And sceptered Monarch with his golden crown;
While near, a fair Maganya woman goes,
Who boasts a huge ring pendant from her nose!

For thee, O Fashion, maidens are confined
By harem's walls, to Nature's wonders blind;
For thee poor babes are wedded ere they grow
To think and love, and Life's great duties know;
For thee the flesh is pierc'd, and fair cheeks scarred,
Art is outrag'd, and Nature's image marred.
Base Fashion! Fiend incarnate! in thy name
The funeral pyre shoots forth its fatal flame;
And there the Indian squaw laments her chief,—
Compelled to die, forsooth, to prove her grief!

Atrocious folly! shameful sin and crime,
That Man should crawl when God would have him climb!
Are we but brainless apes that we should heed
The laws that thou, vile Fashion, hast decreed?
Learn from thee what to do, and eat, and wear?
Borrow our faith, our action, and our prayer?
Be other's echoes? Ne'er use Will or Brain?
Be shackled fools, deform'd and rack'd with pain?
Nay, Goddess! bold and strong in wisdom grown,
We curse thy name, and kneel at Reason's throne!

An Epitaph.

Like flaming comet on a darkened sky,
    A God-sent ray
Streamed through the depths of forest gloom where I
    Groped on Life's way.

I loved the warmth and kissed the golden glow,
    I cried "Oh, stay!"
The sunbeam fled, and left me blackness, woe
    And lifeless clay!

AMBROSE TAYLOR.

The Granite Cliffs at the Land's-End.

Hail, wild Bolerium! where the unceasing shocks
Of earth and ocean clash; where roar and moan
Of furious winds affright the ear! Hail! igneous rocks!
Whose weight would make the fabled Atlas groan;
Whose dormant power would mock at Hercules! Your tops,
Hoar with the age of countless centuries, ye proudly bear
With awing majesty and lofty mien! The grim Cyclops
Ne'er built such walls impregnable as ye uprear
In mighty soaring grandeur! On your highest crests
Those birds of Jupiter, the royal eagles, built their nests!

Your beetling sides give bounds to Neptune's sway;
Your bases are the world's foundation stones;
Your fallen bowlders, bathed in foaming spray,
The stateliest frigates wreck, and strew the bones
Of bravest mariners along the yellow sand
Which sun and shower and frost have crumbled down
From your storm-beaten sides! Your mighty strand
Spurns back the wave's white rage and billow's surge, while down
From dizzy heights ye frown in silent eloquence! Your towers
By Nature shaped and built, heed not Time's fleeting hours!

Ye'll lift your peaks while ages pass away,
And we are traced by relics delved from down
Beneath earth's surface ; just as we to-day
Trace Pompeii's courts, and Herculaneum's town ;
Till that " last day " with mighty noise shall come,
When elements shall melt with fervent heat,
And Earth and all its works receive their doom :
Here will ye stand on adamantine feet !
And when the avenging flames have onward passed,
May help to form another Earth at last !

Tolling out the Old Year and Ringing in the New, 1878—79.

High up in the dim church tower,
At solemn midnight hour,
Tolls forth with startling power
    Loud tenor bell.

As to and fro is swung
Its heavy rolling tongue,
Wherewith is ever rung
    Funereal knell,

From its deep-sounding throat
Booms out a sullen note,
Whose wandering echoes float
    O'er hill and dell.

" Gone," the bell sternly says,
" Gone are Spring's brightest sprays,
Gone is proud Summer's blaze, —
    Each of them gone !

" Gone are leaves, buds, and flowers ;
Gone are weeks, days, and hours ;
Gone, friends that erst were yours, —
    Dear friends are gone !

"Gone, eyes whose radiant beams,
Flashing love's witching gleams,
Conjured wild waking dreams,—
These, too, are gone!"

"Cease, cease, thou maddening bell,
Thy hideous sobs,
That leap out in the stillness of the night
Like demons loosed from hell;
Thy awful throbs
Fill my whole being with a grim affright!

"Is there no word to yell
Save that of "gone;"
No hopeful message sent by kindly fate;
No gentle, soothing swell
To cheer me on;
No joyful news to sonorously relate?"

"Alas!" gasped out the bell,
With quivering surge,
"Not now speak I of any mortal's fate;
Far weightier tale I tell—
I chant the dirge
Of dying Time,—poor *Eighteen Seventy Eight!*"

* * * * *

Ringing in the New.

Once more with sounding strain
The bell peals out again,
But not in tones of pain
As heretofore;

Nor does it sound alone,
For with its own deep tone
Four other bells make known
With differing power

That in the early morn
Another year is born,
For happy and forlorn,
    For rich and poor.

Pour'd from their ringing throats,
In wild, exulting notes,
Out on the night-wind floats
    To listening ear—

" For high, low, great, and small,
In cot or princely hall,
New Year is come for all—
    All hail, New Year!"

Glad tidings such as these,
In changing harmonies,
And swelling symphonies,
    These joy-bells bear.

" Let all the earth be glad;
With smiles each visage clad;
Nor man nor woman sad,
    Nor child repine;

" But Hope fill every breast,
And Faith give Hope deep zest,
And Charity thrice blest
    With Love combine;

" And, with one wide consent,
From earth to heaven be sent
Deep joy at the advent
    Of *Seventy Nine!*

" What though Old Year is dead;
What though his summer's fled;
What though his flowers have laid
    Their blossoms down!

" We ring of New-born Year;
Sweet Spring will soon be here,
And in her arms she'll bear
    Flowers newly blown.

"April shall smile through tears;
  May laugh at April's fears,
  Till ruddy June appears
    And takes May's crown!

"What though chill north-wind blows;
  What though cold Winter's snows
  Earth's dimpled cheeks enclose
    With spotless veil!

"Soon the chill north-wind's doom
  From sunny south shall come,
  And Earth's pale cheeks shall bloom
    At Summer's tale.

"Then, smiling, she will pour
  From her warm bosom's store
  Gifts bright as those of yore
    O'er hill and dale!"

"Oh what a joyous strain
    Your cadence tells!
Sweet harbingers, ring on your melody,
I pray, ring on again,
    And, 'mid your swells,
Hint what my individual fate shall be.

"Say, shall my house be rear'd
    On shifting sands;
On vapoury clouds shall my life's ladder lean;
And shall my goals when near'd
    Prove shadow-lands;
My retrospect, not *Was*, but *Might have been?*"

"These, mortal, rest with you
    To great extent:
Act well your part—therein all honour lies—
And to all trusts be true;
    A life well spent
Shines here on earth—hereafter in the skies."

"Stay, stay, truth-telling bells,
        A moment stay!
I pray you murmur in my listening ear
Low, gentle canticles,
        Wherein convey
Some mention of a maiden very dear.

"Oh! will she ever place
        Her hand in mine,
And with Love's trembling lips say, 'Yes, I will!'
Then, with sweet smiling face,
        Our paths combine,
And by my side climb Life's steep rugged hill?"

"Oh! this we do not know;
        And if we did
We would not tell you such a secret thing:
Love on, and time will show
        What now is hid;
And if Love wins, we'll make the welkin ring!"

Little Nell: An Idyl of Castle Horneck.

One summer's day, with Little Nell,
I wandered in this ferny dell
To where a sparkling cascade fell.

There we sat upon a stone
With moss and ivy overgrown,
And talked and laughed and loved unknown;

And watched the merry sunbeams flash
And dance upon the brooklet's splash,
As down it fell with scattering dash;

And then ran tortuous in and out—
Here and there and round about—
Toying with its speckled trout;

Who, as the silvery stream sped by,
Deftly caught the venturous fly,
Or wanton, gambolled lazily.

G

In this dell we'd often been—
Nelly called it " a fairy scene,"
And her I named "The Fairies' Queen."

We had beguiled the fleeting hours
Idly culling pretty flowers
From hedges, nooks, and silvan bowers.

Nelly spread them on the stone,
Then arranged them one by one
In tasteful manner quite her own.

Then she took the sweet woodbine,
Its tendril ends she did entwine,
And wreathed thereon wild eglantine.

" For whom weave you that wreath so fair ?"
I asked sweet Nell with careless air,
As though for whom I did not care.

And then with playful coquetry
And laughing eyes thus answered she,
" Watch and wait and you will see ! "

The beauteous garland soon was made,
And toyed about in mock parade,
And all its various hues displayed ;

Held aloft and tossed in air ;
Placed upon her auburn hair—
And kissed at last, I do declare !

" Tis for one who loves me true ;
One whom I love dearly too—
Don't look jealous,—'Tis for you !"

* * * * *

Too like her were those flowers,
Cradled in Nature's bowers,
Gathered in sunny hours—

Alas ! they soon did fade ;
Like them, my Nell is dead,
And in the grave is laid.

H. C. SHUTTLEWORTH.

Christmas Dreams.

When earth was bright with the mystic light
    That on childhood's morning gleams,
And Christmas bells were voices of spells
    That touched into life our dreams,
My fancy would paint that kindly Saint
    Who on wings of the midnight flew,
His gifts to shed round the children's bed,—
    And the dream, tho' a dream, was true.

When youth was sped, and fantasy fled
    In the glare of manhood's noon,
Still my heart would greet one vision sweet,
    Thro' the mist of the Christmas moon;
Down a shining stair came a maiden fair,
    O fond was the joy we knew!
It faded away with the waking day,—
    But my glad love-dream was true.

And now I have dreamed of a world redeemed
   From poverty, pain and ill;
Of peace on earth thro' the Blessed Birth,
   For struggle and strife, good-will;—
Though sadly and slow our world doth grow
   Toward the morning where all is new—
God send us heart still to bear our part
   In making the bright dream true!

Cradle Song.

Sleep, darling, sleep;—
The day is worn to rest;
The sun is faint and low;
Silently over the snow
Night comes out of the West;
And the calm-eyed Angels of eventide
Gather about thy cradle-side;
   Sleep, darling, sleep;

Sleep, darling, sleep;—
Father is far away,
The fields are misty and cold,
The year grows faded and old,
All wan is the world and grey;—
But he comes in sleep-time to baby and me,
For the veiled Dream-Angels set all hearts free;
   Sleep, darling, sleep;

Sleep, darling, sleep;—
Joy shall awake with day,
And the year be young again;
From hearts of sorrowing men
Shadows shall flee away,
When the gold-haired Angel of morn shall come,
And over the bright hills bring him home,
   Sleep, darling, sleep.

My Love Loves Me.

'Tis the last bright hour of a magic time,
    The waking close of a summer dream ;
I shall soon be far from the ocean chime,
    From the sleeping hills and the sunlit stream :
And I ever have lingered, loth to part,
    O sweetest of western vales, from thee ;
But I leave thee now with a bounding heart,
    For I know to-day that my love loves me.

From the cornfields, glowing with August bloom,
    From the sea's soft blue, from the wind-swept down,
I go to my lonely London room,
    To the dust and din of the work-worn town :
But a gay farewell to the golden fields,
    And a light adieu to the laughing sea !
All longing to linger passes, and yields
    To the thrill of the thought that my love loves me.

So I cheerly turn me to work again,
    Life runs in its daily round once more ;
But the stress of thought and the sweat of brain
    Have lost the hardness that erst they wore :
For with strange new glory the world is bright,
    That never before was on land or sea ;
And all things move in a mist of light,
    For joy that I know that my love loves me.

I know by the touch of her tell-tale hand,
    I read in the rose-blush bloom of her cheek,
The lore that a lover can understand,
    The wordless language that hearts can speak—
Yet I hunger to hear it in accents low,
    And I look and long for the day to be,-
The golden day when I sure shall know
    From her own true lips that my love loves me.

A Christmas Card.

Where Cornwall's cliffs breast the Atlantic wave,
Lies an old kingdom, deep in surge-swept grave :
A land of wonder, sunk in a sea-sleep,
One day to rise, King Arthur's state to keep.

Still on the mystic marge of that drown'd land
Strange flowers lonely bloom, strange ruins stand ;
And boatmen hear, borne on the calm tide's flow,
Bells of old towers chime faintly far below.

So, deep beneath our stir of workaday strife,
Lie wrecked ideals of diviner life ;
Old hopes, May-promise, faded soon as seen,
The buried Eden-world that might have been.

Buried, not dead : for still in golden hours,
We light on some rare rose of that land's flowers ;
A face, a dream, a song, a hallowed time,
Rings through life's weed and wave a sad glad chime.

Through the sweet visions of this Holy Tide
God send His dearest angel to thy side,
Some leaf from thy lost Paradise to bring,
So touch thy Christmas with the breath of Spring :

Thy dead shall live ! Eden is yet to be :
Faith finds hope's surest pledge in memory ;
The Age of Gold, that o'er earth's morning smiled,
Is no embalméd corpse ; 'tis an Eternal Child.

Poppies among the Corn.

They merrily dance and gaily jaunt
   Their scarlet in saucy scorn,
Heedless of sickle and scythe they flaunt,
   The poppies among the corn.

Alas for the doom that awaits their pride!
   Laid low on the harvest-morn
All withered and dead they are tossed aside,
   Cast out from among the corn.

Little maid of the mill, thou art fresh and fair
   As though of the August born;
With a ribbon of red in thy gold-bright hair,
   Like poppies among the corn.

Don't live like the poppies, sweet maid of the mill,
   Their day has a close forlorn;
For all their scarlet array, sweet maid,
   They are weeds among the corn.

So live in the light of Eternal Day,
   That on God's great Harvest morn
The Angel-reapers may bear thee away
   To be garnered among His corn.

RICHARD BURROW.

Wreckers and Rescuers.

'Twas evening, and the setting sun sank slowly o'er the main,
The twilight deepened into night, the stars shone out again,
The mighty waves were surging high, then dashed with sullen roar
Upon the sharp and rugged rocks which gird the Cornish shore.

Who has not stood high on the cliff and caught the cooling breeze,
Looking with wonder and delight across the rolling seas?
Who has not wished that rocks and caves with cliffs and sands could tell
Of deeds there done in days of yore, and what brave men befell?

'Twas thus I mused one summer night, and spake the thought aloud —
Ye rocks that stand firm and unmoved amid the waters proud,
Will ye not say what men came here two hundred years ago,
And what they thought, and said, and did, whether for weal or woe?

These words I spoke—then paused awhile and listened for reply,
Then up the cliffs from far below came on the breeze a sigh,
Which seemed to tell of evil done, and then a voice at last
Said—Listen! look around, and see the Spirit of the Past.

The scene was changed. Again 'twas night; no stars were to be seen,
The sky with cloud was overcast, no lighthouse sent its gleam
Across the restless ocean wave the mariner to cheer,
And warn him by its friendly light that rocks and shoals were near.

But hark! the stillness of the night was broken by the sound
Of human voices loud and high, and looking quickly round,
A band of dusky forms I saw, while, with a straining ear,
I listened for the reason why they were gathered here.

And one was saying how a ship with cargo rich and rare
Was soon expected in the bay about ten miles from there,
And how as evening shades came on he saw the distant sail
That soon would near this rocky point, helped by the favouring gale.

Then spake the leader of the band to one close standing by,
"Go down the cliff, just half-way down, and swing the lantern high,
Just as a light would look aloft on a vessel under weigh;
We'll grind her timbers on the rocks, then claim her for our prey."

The deed is done ; the lantern high is rocking to and fro,
The watcher on the merchant ship, he sees it come and go ;
With full sail set, no danger fears, he steers the vessel on
Till close before him breakers roar, and then all hope is gone.

" Down with the helm, bring her about !" the frantic
    captain's cry ;
Too late, too late ! she strikes the rocks, the wooden
    splinters fly ;
Crash ! and her timbers, mast and ropes, with sails, complete
    the wreck ;
Wave after wave all pitiless has swept them from her deck.

At dawn next day the coast is strewed with wreckage far
    and near ;
The murderous band with busy hands are all exultant here.
But God is just, and verily they shall have their reward ;
Transgressors shall find out this truth—transgressors way
    are hard.

Oh ! Spirit of the mighty Past, are these the deeds of yore ?
Did men destroy their fellow men, and by false lights allure?
Oh ! rocks and caves, and sands and cliffs,—oh, be for ever
    dumb
Unless of nobler deeds ye tell in days that are to come !

The wheels of Time had swiftly run two hundred years or
    more,
And in a little seaport town on this our Cornish shore
Another scene :—'Twas winter now,—the blinding hail and
    sleet
Before the wind in fitful gusts came sweeping through the
    street.

The sea-foam flew like flakes of snow before the gathering
    gale,
The sea-gull's scream was heard on high, a solemn dirge-like
    wail,
Yet on the beach, drenched through with spray, some fisher-
    men appear,
And, looking seaward, watch a ship with mingled hope and
    fear.

Some three miles off, a gallant barque, by wind and tempest
    tossed,
Is drifting fast with broken mast ; all hope is well nigh
    lost,
For sunken rocks lie in her course, and in a moment more
The signals of distress go up,—they seek help from the
    shore.

" Lads, shall we try it ?" spake their chief. "Yes ! yes !"
    was their reply.
Then turning to their weeping wives, they gently said
    good-bye,—
For God and for humanity, at Duty's trumpet call,
Resolved to save the perishing or at their post to fall.

Launch, launch the lifeboat !—lend a hand,—heave-to, my
    lads,—give way !
And soon the boat like a thing of life is dashing through
    the spray ;
Stout arms are there, brave hearts beat high ; they grasp
    the straining oar,
And then through billows white with foam they leave the
    rugged shore.

Would ye see heroes ? Here they are, not in their coats of
    mail,
No bloody sword is in their hand, no record tells a tale
Of thousands slain upon the field, of widows left to moan,
Of orphans cast upon the world without a friend or home.

God's heroes these—in dangers tried, to bless the world
    they go,—
To lighten human suffering, to lessen human woe.
Their work is done, the boat returns,—" How many saved ?"
    we cry.
" Why all on board ; of all that crew not one is left to die !"

" Whence comes this change ? no wreckers here ! Oh ! boat-
    men, tell us why
You left your homes and little ones, and anxious wives, to try
To save those men upon the deep, to bring them safe to land ?
What hope of a reward had you, pray tell us, gallant band ?"

"Oh, yes; you know when we were lads, our mothers, good,
   kind dames,
They taught us to be brave and true, and that's how comes
   the change.
"All men are brothers," and the Book contains these good
   words too—
"Do unto others as ye would that they should do to you."

Men, fathers, friends, there's work for all upon life's troubled
   sea,
For moral wreckers still abound, cursing humanity;
The world wants men to lend a hand, some shipwrecked
   ones to save;
Go do your best, 'twill not be lost, for God rewards the
   brave!

Voices.

On Cornubia's heath-clothed hills,
When the sun is setting low,
Bathing woodland, field, and sea
In a glorious golden glow,
Nature, clad in Beauty's garb,
Fair and wonderful to see,
Speaks with no uncertain sound
Of its Maker's majesty.

When the day its course has run,
And the lengthening shadows lie
In the valley,—while the bird
Nightly pours its melody;
When the sparkling star-lamps hang,
Diamond-like, from Heaven above,
Speak they not to those who hear
Of their Maker's pledge of love?

When the waving fields of grain,
Bow beneath the whispering breeze,
When the ripening fruits of earth,
Hide amidst the clustering leaves,

When the dews and rain descend
Heaven's pearl-drops to dispense,
Hear the voice to all the earth
Of the Maker's providence.

Wondrous earth and sea and sky,
Sprang from chaos; strange the birth,
Order, beauty, harmony—
Heaven's laws designed for earth.
Mighty Power spake—'twas done;
"Good" declared Eternal Mind.
Flowers, trees, and rolling sun,
Speak His power to mankind.

Yet how heavy are our ears
To these voices as they tell
Of His mind and power and might,
Wisdom vast, unsearchable.
Oh! how darkened are our eyes
To the beaming rays of light,
Heed we not the voice of Truth,
Care not for extended sight?

Why should human spirits dwell
In the caves of fear and doubt,
Cold and lifeless reasoning,
Keeping hope and light without?
Burst the barriers! Look around,
Hear the voice of Faith and Love,—
Beauty, Heaven, and peaceful Hope
Meets the vision. Look above!

Soaring Thought in ages past
Left the sordid paths below,
Rose by Faith's inspiring power,
Caught the truths which angels know,
Tuned the lyre at Heaven's gate,
Brought the strains to earth again,—
Earth yet vibrates with the sound.
Hear we now the sweet refrain.

Mighty voices of the Past
Come from prophet, priest, and seer,
From the holy martyr'd dead,
Ringing through the ages clear.
Work and wait,—let Duty's call
Evermore your watchword be;
He who knows the sparrow's fall
Cares most surely, man, for thee.

Though discordant tones surround,
Creeds and doctrines formed by men,
Truth perverted, error found,
Wrongs triumphant now and then,—
Though the times seem out of joint,
And the world looks all awry,
Truth shall conquer! Hear the voice—
"Right shall triumph by-and-bye!"

R. HEWETT THOMAS.

Music.

Words woven into frenzied fantasies
Strain fiercely to reveal the inner sense
Of all the vast soul feels, in the intense
Strong surging rhythms and deep pulsings, miss
Of all the meaning wrapped in one mute kiss:
Ten thousand songs gain not the recompense
Of hands pressed softly sweet, conveying thence
A world of love surged in a world of bliss.

Until I heard mysterious mutterings
Throb tenderly from 'plaining instruments
Strange mediums from the far spirit world
Hope lured from soul to soul on trembling wings.
When music speaks then love's sweet ravishments
Lie all before us as a scroll unfurled.

The Savant.

As experts tasked to read a written page
Torn in a thousand shreds, with eager care
Collect and re-arrange until the bare
Truth stands revealed,—even so the sage
Of Nature cons each sign though bleared with age ;
He gathers all earth's mysteries to compare
Her foul contortions with her beauteous fair,
And thereby doth a sapient thirst assuage
To test the written Truth with Truth revealed
In God's own sure handwriting, words direct,
Freed from mediums of man's misgiving tongue,
And when the glorious record all unsealed
Spreads out a fair and noble retrospect
Not vain have savants probed and poets sung.

Love.

The sweet embodiment of an ideal,
Of vague desires and hazed unconscious yearnings
Suddenly shapened, the soul's inconstant turnings
At once transfixed ; of all that sense doth feel
In mute mysterious glimmerings, nor reveal
By any mode of thought's constrained discernings
In channels of wrought words, and mystic burnings
Imaged and transfused to form's semblative seal :
Nay, these poor similies strained to construe
The soul's fine sense that will not brook expression,
A sense that will not mate with reasoned sense,
And that of truth's proud utt'rance proved untrue
By utterings of the soul's unheard confession—
Love-speech impelling we know not where nor whence.

Beauty.

GREAT nature is a mirror that reflects
The mind within : all shapes of loveliness
Answer but faintly to the inward stress
Of that high sense of beauty that directs
Our wandering thoughts to pure and sweet effects ;
And thus she dangles with a sweet caress
The tender flowers, foundlings that gently press
Against our busy pondering, that rejects
All gracious forms until grace thus reminds,
Only the sensual lust of greed and gain
Blossom uncultured in our hearts, exempt
Of beauty's image, that but seldom finds
A place where grosser musings flow amain
And where unlovely thoughts are free to tempt.

Beethoven.

HE breathed into his art the living soul
Of a true sympathy, that quick impelled
The utterance of ennobled thoughts that swelled
In mystic harmonies. The thunder-roll
Of proud defiance scorned the control
Of any fate that fought in vain. Love swelled
From out his heart in melodies that held
The ear in strained desire to sip the whole
Of life and love. Reason is here subdued
By that fine inner instinct that explains
The wondrous meanings that the worlds include
Of here and the hereafter, and regains
The vigour of a lapsing life renewed,
And all the worth of all worth's power attains.

Opening Chorus from
"The Tournament,"
A Comic Opera, by R. Hewett Thomas.

[CHORUS OF SOLDIERS.]

We are warriors bold and daring,
    Fierce our faces, fierce our actions ;
Without any malice bearing
In a manner most unsparing
    We reduce our foes to fractions
With a reckless, restless raging
Fearless fury fuming, waging
Bleared blood broadcast, thus engaging
    Custom smooths these grim transactions,
Only gore our thirst assuaging—
    Peace for us has no attractions.

[*Solo Voice (Bass)*] To a pulp we soon construe them
    Merely for the sake of fighting,
Though our hearts may yearn unto them
In good fellowship we strew them
    In a mincemeat uninviting
    On the plain, without exciting
    Any low or angry feeling;
    'Tis bad form to be revealing
    Any low, revengeful feeling.

[*Chorus of Girls.*] We are maidens prim and prude, O,
    Phosy priestesses and pensive ;
Wanton wiles shall ne'er intrude, O,
In our bosoms all subdued, O,
    In our bosoms apprehensive ;
    Yet our yearnings are extensive
    For the vast incomprehensive—
That's the reason we're endued, O,
    With these feelings apprehensive,
Lest perchance in amorous mood, O,
Wanton whispers might intrude, O,
In our bosoms unsubded, O.

[*Solo Voice (Soprano)*]   So when gallants come a-wooing
　　With their leering and their sighing,
　We their passions soon construing
　Bind us not to our undoing.
　　Nay, our hearts are not complying
　　To love's pretty prattling lying,
　Nor quaint rhymes shall ever win us,
　Nor the stories that ye spin us,
　Senile sonnets shall not win us,
　　We are learned and æsthetic
　And we hate war's vulgar glory :
　　We are only sympathetic
　　With the humidly pathetic,—
　We abhor your battles gory.

[*Chorus of Soldiers.*]   Stout and valiant, quick and furious,
　　Stirring peace should she be napping,
　　　Quiet times are most injurious,
　　　For a sense unique and curious
　To our hearts comes tipping, tapping,
　　Rough and rushing, fierce and furious ;
　Still we hear the restless rapping
　Like a flag's continuous flapping,
　'Tis only love that comes a-tapping
　　Though we hoped it might prove spurious ;
　　'Tis vexatious and most curious
　　Loud the rapping grows and furious.

[*Chorus of Girls.*]   Well, we might concede your passion
　In a mild platonic fashion
　　If you would forsake your fighting
　　For a pastime less exciting,
　Such as, when the evening closes,
　Twine us eglantine and roses ;
　　When the evening calm and still is
　　Worship sun flowers and fair lilies.

CHARLES L. FORD.

Resolution.

Take thy side! around thee raging
    Rolls the battle through the land;
All thy comrades are engaging:
    Who art thou, aloof to stand?

Take thy side! the world's whole story
    Is the strife of man with man;
Strive thine utmost, best, and glory
    To be called a partisan.

Take thy side! and, having taken,
    Play thy part, erect and brave;
Like the steadfast oak unshaken,
    Though the tempest round thee rave.

Act the good thy thought conceiveth;
    What though some should misconstrue?
To the spirit that achieveth
    Highest honour is to do.

Leave to meaner minds the wooing
    Of the multitude's applause;
Glory crowns the glorious doing
    By irrevocable laws.

Shrink not if thy feebler brothers
    Shout, "What will this dreamer say?"
Nor, to keep the smile of others,
    Fling thine own esteem away.

For the honour or disfavour
    Swerve not; count not loss or gain;
'Till the pliant herd that waver
    Turn and follow in thy train.

Bear a dauntless heart; inherit
    All that to this right doth cling;
For the resolute of spirit
    Is alone both lord and king.

Therefore let no light thought move thee
    From the deed thy soul hath planned;
Forward in thy might, and prove thee
    Of the nobles of the land.

The Iceberg.

FAR from the land where the north-winds blow,
From the cities of ice and the fields of snow,
I float and drift with the ocean's flow.

From the sunny south the warm winds play,
And my heart it wasteth day by day,
And melts in tears on its joyless way;

For I pass the hills where the pine-woods cling,
And I scent the breath of the budding spring,
But my bosom is bare of the tiniest thing

That hath colour or life; and the little bird blest
That lighteth a moment her wings to rest
Bringeth no mate, and buildeth no nest.

I glide by the huts where the fishers dwell,
But they curse my steps, for they know full well
How keen are the airs that round me swell.

And the mariner steers his craft with care,
Nor seeketh a port in my island fair,
For he whispers, " The angel of death is there."

All rosy bright are the hues that show
On my topmost peak in the sunrise glow—
But the heat ne'er causeth the corn to grow.

And my crystal walls their lustre fling
Like a palace of gems for a fairy king—
But a blade of grass were a brighter thing.

And fearful and grand is the long rebound
Of the thunder-crash when the ice splits round—
But the song of a bird were a sweeter sound.

So I journey on, through sun or cloud,
Silent and cold, and lofty and proud,
Like a lonely heart in a loveless crowd;

And I weep, I weep, in my yearning vain
For warmth and life, as in mist and rain
I float and drift o'er the widening main;

Till I find the path of the warm wide stream
That glows in the kiss of the tropic beam,
And melt and fade like a baseless dream.

Pupilage.

O CHILD as yet, who canst not read
    The record by thy Father penned,
Forbear to shout thy hasty creed,
    Till thou canst further comprehend;
The book lies open, but the whole
    Eludes thy search, while, one by one,
Leaf after leaf the mighty scroll
    Unfolds, till all is done.

Hear, but with reverence ; voices fall
    Around thee from the eternal shore ;
Some thou mayst reach—thou canst not all,
    Though fain, and pondering more and more :
Yet hoard them in thy secret heart,
    As children grasp whate'er they can,
Till twilight pass, and knowledge start
    To broad noon in the man.

Teach, but with meekness, as a child
    Leading his brother by the hand
To their far home across the wild
    By starlight, in a wintry land :
Learn still from whom thou teachest ; give,
    And, giving, ever more receive :
Scorn not the meanest ; lowly live,
    And loftiest things achieve.

Think life is larger than the bound
    Of fourscore years ; death but a stone
That marks thy travel ; heaven the round
    Of glorious deeds when thou art grown
Beyond thy tasks and playthings ; fame
    A higher meed than men's applause ;
Evil, good's foil and shadow : shame
    Nought, save for broken laws.

Love, or thou liv'st not ; life is more
    Than counts by pulses : make thy gain
Thy brother's welfare, so thy store
    Shall prosper, nor thy work be vain :
Walk where thy Master bids thee ; shun
    No rough path, or deservéd rod :
Right up the sunbeam seek the sun,—
    God's light must lead to God.

Souvenirs.

Thy light-brown hair before me lies,
  But thou art far away,
In the calm bowers of Paradise,
  Where sainted spirits stray;
And richer curls adorn thy brow,
  And stars bestrew thy hair;
And angels are thy comrades now,
  Thyself an angel there.

I touch the faded cypress leaf,
  And back returns again
The hour of pain, the night of grief
  When thou didst pass from men;
I see the grave's new-opened mould,
  The path by mourners trod;
But life's full joys for thee unfold
  In the bright land of God.

Come down to-night—the hour is thine,—
  And sit some while with me,
And sing me some sweet song divine
  That angels sing to thee;
And tell me all—how saintly fair
  Thy ordered home on high;
Life's burden teach like thee to bear,
  And teach like thee to die.

Pass quickly on, ye lingering years
  As the swift shuttle, flee!
Bring the long rest from griefs and fears,
  The grave's sweet sleep to me!
Sleep to my dust, but life and light
  To my glad soul above,
With her, the good, the fair, the bright,
  The maiden of my love.

Life.

We blow away rose petals with light breath
    'Mid funeral knells;
We stand upon the shore of the ocean, death,
    And gather shells.

Wave after wave rolls in, and sweeps away
    Sister and brother;
We miss their smiles, yet cease not from our play,
    Choosing another.

One hour the homely task, the vulgar round
    Of loss and winning;
The next, God's light, the prospect without bound,
    New life's beginning.

Prisoned we lie in this Circean cell,
    Our true selves loathing,
Till Death strikes o'er us, by his heaven-taught spell,
    Right mind and clothing.

As children ne'er outside their native sod
    Dream not of ocean,
We reck not of the far off hills of God,
    At ease in Goshen.

A light has shone amidst our darker ways,
    A voice has spoken;
And lo! the long unchanging round of days
    Sudden is broken.

In the smooth chain of life one flaw appears,
    Spoiling succession;
The wise men listen, but their baffled ears
    Boast not possession

Of this one secret—binding all beside
    By weight and measure,
Searching all mysteries else, till nature hide
    Nought from their pleasure.

Yet this, earth's riddle evermore unguessed,
    On order jarring,
This, the one chord untuned amid the rest,
    Earth's music marring,—

This is the hand let down, the unclosed door,
    The whispered warning;
This is the light that shines our feet before
    Unto the morning.

And so we walk as princes in disguise,
    Mean of condition,
The everlasting hidden from our eyes
    By thin partition,

Ready each moment at some weaker seam
    To burst asunder,—
Till all eternity across our dream
    Roll as the thunder.

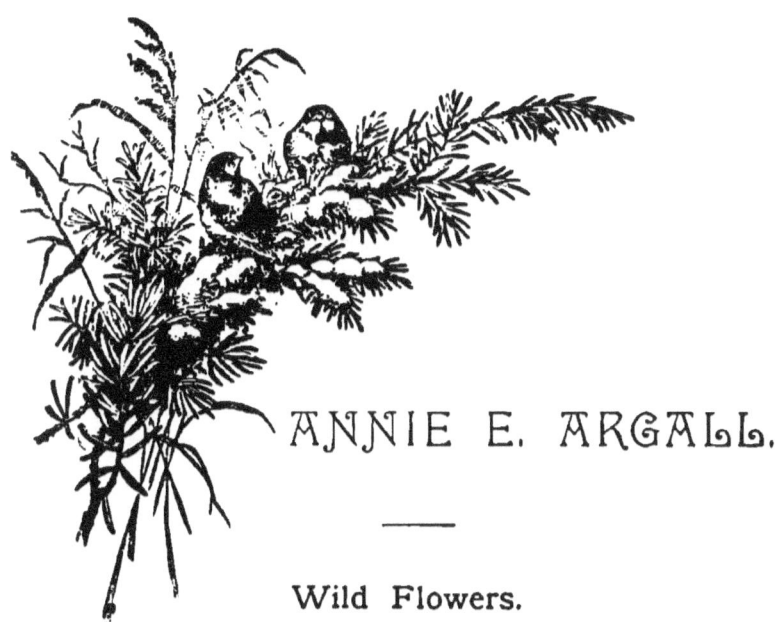

ANNIE E. ARGALL.

Wild Flowers.

A LOVELY bouquet of wild treasures they brought me,
Fresh and sweet from the hedgerow, the marsh, and the brake,
Which lavish such fragrance and brightness around me
That I cannot but love them for fair Beauty's sake.

Osmunda! thou king of all ferns, celebrated
And long-honoured by minstrel in ballad and rhyme,
How welcome thy shade near the cool, rippling streamlet,
'Neath the tall leafy trees in the warm summer-time.

Not less art thou welcome 'mid orchis and iris,
Brilliant blossoms, thy emerald beauty to grace;
And with more of thy kin, though none like thee so royal,
Is the tall, stately foxglove in dignity's place.

Fair starred marguerita and sweet honeysuckle
Nestle closely together in mutual bliss,
And the frail briar-roses with pure perfumed petals
To my fancy seem fit for an angel's soft kiss.

Yet far more do I love them, the sweet silent flow'rets,
For the message of patience and love which they bear,
A God-given example of trust in His mercy,
A full proof that our Father for all things doth care.

The Flower-Star of Spring.

Oh ! why do they call thee the emblem of sadness,
Pale, sweet, modest primrose, ah ! canst thou say why ?
When our eager glance rests on thy fair soothing beauty,
And we willingly gather thy morsels of fragrance ;
Is aught in that beauty to sadden the eye,
Or cast down our spirits, or call forth a sigh ?

No, not when we plucked thee, as free and light-hearted
We joyously rambled through woodland and dell ;
Quite content to exist in the joy of the moment,
All enrapt with our simple discernment of nature,
Uncritical, pleasing, heigho ! we know well
The pleasures of childhood we grasped ere they fell.

Is part of thy mission, fair primrose, beloved,
To bring to remembrance the days of lost youth ?
Oh, is this the lone cause of the mist o'er our vision,
And the tear trembling over the sad drooping eyelash ?
Aye, utter it softly, but whisper the truth,
If grace may incline to a thing so uncouth.

But, blossom, we miss now the pride of thy beauty ;
As resting in state on the däis of green,
Thou hast budded and bloomed in thy fair woodland palace
While distributing gifts in a measure unbounded,
Sweet miniature sovereign, thy kingdom we ween
Is spacious to boast such a shy little queen.

To-day we admire, although in thy dominion
To trace willing footsteps falls not to our share ;
It may be that we traverse the streets of a city,
'Mid the whirl of its turmoil and business-like pressure,
And read thy sweet message displayed even there ;
What wonder, that reading, a sigh moves the air ?

The sadness is transient, a fleeting emotion,
But not the less truly a genuine regret ;
Those the brightest and best of the days of our spring-time,
With the years are now passing for once and for ever ;
Ah ! primrose, their memory we would not forget,
And thus for remembrance, fair flow'r, we have met.

A Convict's Baby.

"He's dying!" then shortly they add, "He is dead!"
But never a tear o'er the still form is shed.
And why? It were folly to grieve at his gain,
The poor child who had borne such a life of pain,
And well do they know it, those folks we term "hard,"
As they calmly discuss "the poor little card."

Yes, dead! Of neglect and starvation he died,
For want of the care which we Christians denied.
"We never refused!" do I hear all around?
No; we only pass heedless where sorrows abound,
Reproaching the poor who lack leisure to weep
O'er the baby who rests in his last sweet sleep.

But wan faces light up as the words pass on—
"He died of starvation,—the baby has gone!"
Bleared eyes grow more fiery, rough tones become loud,
Till it ends in an angry, riotous crowd,
All fiercely demanding redress of their wrongs,
Asserting the right which to England belongs.

There are cries of "A riot!" policemen march out,
And speedily put the insurgents to rout.
The leaders are led to the gaol one by one,
A result of the death of the factory-girl's son;
The police do their duty, receive their reward,
But, ah! can that baby's frail life be restored?

His father? a felon of noted ill-fame;
Yet should the child starve for his parents' bad name?
His mother is only a convict's young wife,
Who once helped her husband to save his weak life.
An "accomplice" finds work so hard to procure;
How great is the struggle to live and endure!

So th' baby was starved, while our guardians stand by
And proclaim that the workhouse is always nigh,
That wife was a mother with fond loving heart,
Who felt that she could not so readily part
With her only child. But, alas! for her grief,
Her babe has now passed beyond earthly relief.

She was willing to toil, and did her work well,
But her wage was a fraud, her workroom a hell;
The girl-wife and mother was honest and brave,
Yet her baby now lies in a starveling's grave;
She carries a grief-stricken heart in her breast,
But her toil must go on without change, without rest.

The sigh of that mother, the wail of her boy,
Shall mingle for ever with anthems of joy.
May they reach every heart, that we all may hear,
From the tradesman's lad to the cynical peer,—
That desolate sigh, and the starving child's moan,
As they blend with the rioters' sullen groan,

Till all, moved by pity and love, are impelled
To stop the oppression and tyranny held
Over workmen by masters, by rich over poor,
To grant bread to the wee hungry babes who implore
By their weak, feeble cries, the succour and aid
Of every true parent our Maker hath made.

Chrysanthemums.

Chrysanthemum!
The season's latest trophy, thee we hail
With rapturous ecstasy. Thy many tints
Are varied as the rainbow's beauteous hues;
Or, as the glowing sky at break of day,
In morning splendour wrapt. Can aught excel
Thy pure and snowy blossoms, wondrous fair,
And those bright golden gems so freely poured
Upon us by the Autumn's brilliant sun,
Assisted by a frequent copious shower
Of soft refreshing rain? Thy purple blooms
Could vie with any ancient regal robes
Of solemn grandeur and of sumptuous state;
Or with the vaporous mantle which enfolds
The hills when morning dawns. Thy crimson flowers

Can only be compared with sunset's glow
And the deep lustre of the ruby fair
Caught by a passing ray of glittering light
Or golden sunbeam. All our flowers are sweet,
But none more dear than thee, Chrysanthemum,
Blooming when they are faded, when the wind
Plays ruthlessly among the coloured balls,
Tossing them here and there with fierce, rough glee,
Yet adding to their strength. But words are vain
To speak of all thy brilliant lights and shades.
The glowing picture of the garden, gay
With thy bright blossoms, numberless and rare,
Is ever better seen than thus described.
Farewell, we whisper. While the wild wind blows
Bloom on in hardy beauty, lovely strength,
Our latest autumn star, Chrysanthemum.

Our sweet English Rhine—the Fal.

O, LOVELY Fal, whose wooded banks
To thy fair self give wondrous grace,
Of thee, loved stream, I fain would speak,
And having power, thy path would trace,
As flowing onward day by day,
Gently thou glidest on thy way.

Thou, changing ever, yet the same
To me, whose memory loves to rove
Along thy winding silvery course;
Around thy path I oft have wove
Sweet thoughts of pleasures past and gone,
When Love's fair sunlight o'er me shone.

As I, in frail and simple craft,
Down on thy heaving breast did glide;
In the glad transport of those hours
I dreamt not of what might betide,—
I had no thought for care or grief,
Or that life's joys would be but brief.

But those were days that now are past,
Though ling'ring in my memory yet,
Sweet joyous hours of honeyed bliss
That could I, I would ne'er forget,
For they are graven on my heart,
And in my dreams still bear a part.

List! gentle river, to my song,
And bear it onward to the sea;
Accept the tribute I would bring,
The meed of praise I grant to thee.
Flow on, O Fal, with this refrain,
Ye rippling waves, take up the strain.

Our Rocky Cornish Coast.

LOUDLY sounds the breakers' roar,
Dashing 'gainst the rocky shore,
Whirling eddies to the fore,
   Backed by rolling surge.

Rising, falling, wreathed in white,
Swelling, foaming, as with spite,
On they rush with awful might,
   To the cliffs' steep verge;

Overwhelming with their spray,
Precipice so rough and grey,
Then receding, mocking, gay,
   Toward the open sea.

SAM. J. WILLIAMS.

Raise the Flag of Resolution.

When the fair winds of Life's morning
   Waft the fragrance of its flowers
From the fields with bloom adorning,
   All to beautify bright hours,
Raise the flag of resolution
   On the road of Truth and Right,
Till the sun of evolution
   Banish doubt with new-born light.

Raise the standard high, ye people,
   Impregnated with its fire—
Like the vane on yonder steeple—
   In the vanguard of desire;
Pressing forward, never yielding,
   Though the strife rage loud and long,
Still the weaker brother shielding
   From the cruel and the wrong.

Raise the royal banner ever,
   'Tis a forecast of the free,
Weaved with cords we dare not sever
   From the heart's sincerity;
Wave it wide o'er paths of glory,
   Where determined men pursue,
Tell it out in song and story
   Resolution is to *do*.

Bear the banner long and lasting
   Till the clarion notes of praise
Through Time's arches ever casting
   Mould its truths for future days;
With resolve stamped on the features
   Carry out each noble theme,
And remember we are creatures
   Born to do, not vainly dream.

The Golden Age.

If each his destined duty did
   In sunshine and in shower,
This world would be a blest abode,
   And life a golden hour.

The land would lose its idle drones,
   The soul forget its sorrow,
Toiling in tranquil hope to-day
   To realise to-morrow.

Then helping hands would be out-held
   By willing sons of labour
To smooth the rude and rugged path
   Of every needy neighbour.

The prison-house would shattered fall,
   The workhouse lose its paupers,
While homes would boast of noble sons
   And lowly Virtue's daughters.

Then mighty minds, all shaped in truth,
  Would guide the people ever,
Leading to light beyond the gloom,
  To drudge in darkness never.

The reaper's song at harvest time,
  Like peals of laughter ringing,
Would echo through the vernal vales
  While sheaves were homeward bringing.

Country with country would combine,
  And prove by arbitration
The human throng one brotherhood,
  One people, and one nation.

The Blind Boy's Lament.

O TELL me not the lovely light
  No more my eyes shall greet
From distant hills when day awakes
  Life's story to repeat;
And as it spreads its golden path
  Across the waters blue,
Must I, all sightless, sit me still,
  And miss that radiance too?

O tell me not my days must be
  As dense as darkest night,
To hear glad sounds and not to see
  The source of their delight,—
To hear my old companions tell
  Of pleasures on the wing,
And not to see each happy face
  Aglow with joys they bring.

Shall I not see the flowers that bloom,
  The blossoms on the thorn,
With fragrance rich and juicy sweet,
  With dewdrops of the morn?
Shall I not see the lark again
  Rise from his lowly bed,
Trilling a carol to the sky
  With little wings outspread?

O tell me not my books must be
  Unopened in the case,
That I no more at eventide
  Their flowing lines shall trace;
O tell me rather, like yon glow,
  The light of my dear eyes
But for awhile in darkness sets
  In glorious dawn to rise.

A Song of Labour.

We want not leaders insincere,
  Whose schemes abortive cast,
Change fruitful fields to barren wastes,
  Like Autumn's dreary blast.

Men of heroic heart we want
  To stand on Discord's tomb,
And plant the true Sincerity
  In all its lovely bloom.

We want the energetic tact,
  The inward breathing fire,
The pluck and push which makes a man
  Upraise his morals higher.

We want the soul-ennobling themes,
  The cream of manly thought,
The architecture of design
  In all its cunning taught.

We want the sure progressive art,
    The hope-inspiring song,
The ever practical and right
    To overcome the wrong.

We want the sympathetic word,
    With Mercy's gentle hand,
To pioneer the people's cause
    Throughout the English land.

Go Feed the Birds.

Go feed the birds, my brothers, go,—
    They perish by the way;
The winds are keen and they are weak;
    O feed them now, I pray,
And scatter broadcast on the ground
    In wood and meadow there
The little crumbs of charity
    With tenderness and care.

Go feed the birds, my brothers, now,
    Out through the snow and sleet,
With mercy in thy heart and hand,
    Strew wide the welcome meat;
They twitter as they hop along,
    Poor little homeless things,
With strength near gone they scarce can fly,
    Or use their puny wings.

Go feed the little feathered flocks,
    They're tamed by want and frost,—
O strew the fragments ye may have,
    Nor let a crumb be lost;
Go with a loving mind each morn
    Till wintry days are done,
When their glad notes shall tell of praise
    Beneath a summer sun.

Through Meadows Green.

How sweet to roam through meadows green,
  Above the sun a-shining,
To tread the lovely flowery sheen,
  Within glad thoughts divining;
To wander on without a care,
  Or hate or harm the heart to share.

To see the river gliding on,
  Gurgling, tinkling by the way,
As if a-hasting to be gone
  Where briny ocean holds the sway,
Whose foaming white doth fringe the land
  Along the coast from strand to strand.

To watch the bee go humming by,
  Made joyous from the juicy herb;
To hear the lark up to the sky
  Go winging with his song superb,
Till thought and feeling in their flight
  With brighter natures do unite.

To hear the chorus of the birds
  Burst forth in answer to the song,
Which tells of nature without words
  Polluted by the human throng,
Till valley, meadow, from above
  Seem like the very haunts of love.

E. L. T. HARRIS-BICKFORD.

Lander's Grave.

"English people in general, and Cornish and Truro people in particular, will be grieved and surprised to learn that the precise spot in which the great African Explorer, LANDER, lies buried at Fernando Po, cannot be identified. A short inscribed tombstone was erected to his memory, but it appears to have been uncared for, and the result is that the tropical vegetation, in the midst of which it was placed, has completely overgrown it."

AND is thy grave with jungle overgrown?
   And may no eye detect thy place of rest?
Canst thou not call some sheltered spot thine own,
   With flowers bright blooming o'er thy dauntless breast?

Martyr! I marvel as I think of thee,
   Removed from loving kindred and from home,
And wonder greatly how such thing can be,
   Afar, afar, across the whitening foam!

And must it thus continue? Dearth be thine?
   Are there no hearts that beat to make the spot
That holds thee beautiful? no thought benign
   Yet to be born to crown thy hapless lot?

Chief of thy time! of valorous enterprise!
  Much gentle kindness should be shown to thee;
Dear should thy grave be to all English eyes,
  And Cornish hearts, alive to chivalry!

Thy life was lost, investigation-led,
  Thy brave heart burned to open up new ways;
Death only claimed thy clay,—thou art not dead,
  Though closed on earth the sunshine of thy days.

And those who cherish men like Davy, Drake,
  Drew, Howe, and Raleigh, should not let thee lie
Supinely comfortless, but thought awake
  How best to draw to thee the passing eye.

Though sleeping far from Cornwall, Cornwall's son,
  In History's page thy name is graven deep,
Not midst thine own, but foes amid, were won
  Those laurels bright 'twas thine to form and keep!

And O! I trust such feeling yet will stir
  In Cornish hearts as shall re-echo wide,
And prove that thou hast many a worshipper
  Whose heart, at thought of thee, doth swell with pride.

God guard thee, Lander! in thy slumber lone,
  And breed the wish to re-invest thy grave
With fitting monument of carven stone,
  Near Santa Isabel—across the wave!

When Mother's Smile was Lost to Me.

When mother's smile was lost to me
  I cared not for the sun;
When mother's love was lost to me
  Then hopes died one by one;
I felt within a world of thorns,
  No flowers to greet the sight;
The heart that once a mother mourns
  Beats sadder in its might.

Hers was the gentle voice that spake
    Like music to my soul,
Hers, tenderest words that keep awake
    Best thoughts on Memory's scroll ;
Her cheerful spirit made more glad
    The home she used to queen
Ere bitter sorrow made her sad
    Amid a blighted scene.

How much I miss her tender care
    No pen of mine can say ;
Her image haunts me everywhere,
    By night as well as day,
Just as she used to be she seems
    In memory to me now,
Presiding over all my dreams,
    And kissing my sad brow.

Burns.

POET-MAGICIAN, who, with marvellous hand,
    Taught Scotland's sons the witchery of song,
    Whose tongue—the outlet for a spirit strong—
Sung rapturously of love and native land
In numbers wild, inspiriting, and grand ;
    Thy native hills re-echo still thy strain,
    Resounding loud o'er ceaseless, moving main
To wheresoe'er a Scottish son doth stand !

Ah ! matchless prince of northern minstrelsy,
    Whose bosom heaved with ecstasy divine,
O that more bards could strike the lyre like thee,
    Or that one half thy priceless gift were mine :
Then might I trust with some just hope to be
    Far nearer that deep pulsing thrill of thine.

When I No More.

WHEN I no more on earth shall sigh and shiver
  Beneath the chill that coldly sweepeth there ;
When lo ! my spirit shall have crossed the river
  To breathe the balsam of a purer air :
Will no one tread where green the grass grows o'er me,
  And some dear bird its requiem sings close by ?
When earth, that once so glowing spread before me,
  No more hath magic for my curtained eye ?

Will any tender thought be cast upon me ?
  Will any loving hand bedeck my bed ?
Will any misty eye look earthward on me,
  And think of songs and words I've sung and said ?
Will little daises peep and peer above me ?
  And grass-blades (sheathless swords) protect my rest ?
Will leafy boughs seem bending o'er to love me,
  And look down calmly on my silent breast ?

Ah ! yes, I know that Nature still will lend me
  Those fair sweet things that cheered my path on earth ;
And kindly boughs lean o'er me and defend me,
  And streams have courses round me,—flowers have birth ;
And I will see them from a higher station,
  And chant their praises from a higher world ;
And spend my time in hymning God's creation,
  A new sphere opened, and woe's standard furled !

The Student's Appeal to Art.

TRANSCENDENT, seated on her sapphire throne,
  Gleams Art, resplendent o'er a conquered world ;
She spells mankind and calls them all her own,
  And wide beneath the sun her flag's unfurled ;
  Her eyes stream starry light, her brow is pearled
And garlanded with wreath of myrtle green,
  And at her shapely feet lies Love, close-curled,
Whilst beauty all around illumes the scene,
And sheds connecting lights her glinting locks between !

O glorious Art! expressive as the skies
  When kingly Sun with potent force appears;
Spelled by the lustre of thy speaking eyes—
  Supreme the memory that thy glory rears,
Thy brow will ne'er be dulled by flight of years,
But ever beam as beaming now, benign!
And be thou kissed by Joy, or bathed in tears,
Proud is the heart that aye can beat with thine,
And paint, and carve, and sing, and raptured call thee "fine!"

Thus would I crave one boon, one little boon
  Transcendent Art, give heed unto my prayer;
And though thou see not fit to grant it soon,
  Till I still further climb thy golden stair,
  If thou but smile on me, I'll not despair,
Not though sad troubles congregate around,
  But dream and do, and do and dream, and dare,
And be when wrapped by thee, by bravery bound,
Nor shall a truer heart than mine to thee be found.

And this is all I ask: wilt give me "nay"?
  Ah! no, I feel thy answer, ere thy tongue
Soft syllables the all-creating "aye,"
  Thou wouldst not that my knell of death were rung;
  And I will sing again as I have sung,
Though strengthened by the faith I have in thee,
  And through the bee-cares that have seized and stung,
I—I will forward go,—go forward, free,
And front the frowning height, and dare thy brave son be.

And thus, fair goddess! lay I at thy feet
  My strict allegiance, and my sacred trust;
And pray thee make in me thy powers complete,
  Ere heart shall cease to beat and brain be dust;
  Somehow I feel within this much I must,
Though falt'ring, feeble, child-like, immature;
  And ere old age shall clothe me in its rust,
Be mine to breed some thoughts that shall endure,
Some thoughts that, born of thee, shall make Fame's throne
    secure!

JENNIE HARRY.

Harvest Thanks.

HEAVENLY Father listen now,
    From Thy throne above,
To the praises sung below
    Of thy tender love.

Love for us in all things good
    Thou hast shown again:
Fields are bright with golden corn
    For the wants of men.

Reapers, with their sickles bright,
    In the harvest fields,
Gather in the waving grain
    Which the kind earth yields.

We had doubted when the rain
    Ceaselessly did fall,
Thinking not that One above
    Careth for us all.

O forgive our doubting hearts ;
   Give us faith to see
Thou art wise, and true, and good ;
   May we trustful be.

Man may work from morn till night,
   Scattering tiny seed ;
Yet if Thou withhold Thy hand
   Sore would be man's need !

Then let praises fill the earth
   And the skies ascend,
Till to catch the reaper's song,
   Angels listening bend ;

Bend, as if the earth-struck lyre
   Found in heaven a chord ;
While the myriad hosts proclaim
   Praise unto the Lord !

Hope.

I sit by the restless ocean
   And watch the dashing waves,
As they chase each other madly
   And break in the open caves.

The bold cliffs are high and rugged,
   Each side of the little bay ;
Where I saw from a Cornish headland
   My lover's ship sail away.

I fancy I still can see him,
   With his eyes of deepest blue,
And hear him say—" Farewell, lassie,
   I'll soon return to you."

That would-be " soon " seems a lifetime,
   Two years have passed away,
But my boy has sent no missives
   To cheer me day by day.

But something my heart is thrilling
    When thinking of the past,
'Tis the hope that springs eternal
    When the die of love is cast.

That fond hope nerves my spirit
    And lightens all my way;
When despair my path would darken
    Hope makes it bright as day.

And I'll sit and watch the billows
    Until my eyes shall fail,
Gazing across the ocean
    At each vessel's fluttering sail.

KITTIE JULEFF.

The Setting Sun.

I stood at the door one evening,
    Watching the setting sun
As it passed away in glory,
    After its work was done.

Its glorious rays were shedding
    A glow o'er hill and dale,
Caressing the mountains lofty,
    Kissing the lowest vale.

Lower and lower 'twas sinking
    Into the crimson west,
And methought 'twas like the Christian
    Going to eternal rest.

Thus would I go into glory,
    Into the realms of day;
Where Christ is the bright sun shining,
    Whose rays ne'er pass away.

The Bride.

To my Friend on the occasion of her Marriage.

I CANNOT let thee leave to-day
    Thy childhood's happy home,
Without a prayer that peace and love
    May ever with thee roam.

I see thee in thy shining robes
    Bright as the morning sun,
About to take the solemn vows
    That bind two hearts as one.

What future has in store for thee
    Thou surely canst not tell,
But if love reigns within thy heart
    Thou wilt be guarded well.

For she will soften ev'ry care,
    And scatter fragrance sweet
Upon the stormy waves of life
    Which thou, dear, mayest meet.

May Peace in all her beauty spread
    A calm on ev'ry strife,
And make thee bear with fortitude
    The holy name of wife.

And when the sunshine of thy youth
    Falls gently on the wane,
May he who calls thee his to-day
    Renew his vows again;

Whilst thou, with ev'ry wifely art,
    Wilt evermore devise
Some little plan for making home
    A second Paradise.

Childhood.

Oh! the happy days of childhood,
   How I wish them back again;
Free from sorrow, care and trial,
   Knowing naught of grief or pain.
Like a calm and happy valley,
   Where the crystal waters flow,
In a soft perpetual motion,
   Making music here below.

Loving mem'ries sweep now o'er me,
   Bringing back those days of yore;
Making me forget my sadness,
   And I seem at home once more;
Yes! at home 'mid all the dear ones,
   Underneath a mother's care,
Taking to her all our trials,
   Sure of finding solace there.

Peaceful, happy vale of childhood,
   Angels surely lingered there,
Watching o'er each tiny flower
   With such tender, zealous care:
Oh! ye angels of the children,
   Will ye not pass here to-day?
And forgetting I'm a woman
   Drop a blessing on the way.

JOHN PASCOE.

Penseroso.

Those tender ties are sundered now,—
    This heart is doomed to die;
Vain is the oft-repeated vow,
    And vain the pensive sigh;
The morning breaks so lone and sad
    Upon my wakeful eye,
And I have none to make me glad
    Beneath the sunlit sky.

O! tell me where sweet comfort flows,
    And where the cheering beams?
Sweet solace for these latent woes,
    And living crystal streams?
And where is love, unchanging love,
    Love that can never die?
Not on this earth; 'tis formed above,
    In fairer climes on high!

Once I had love, so pure and fair,
    With all its blissful charms,
A youthful heart mine own to share,
    And soft enfolding arms,
And ruby lips, and flashing eyes,
    And light and nectar flowed
Whene'er we met beneath those skies
    Which o'er us brightly glowed.

In sheltered nook, in balmy grove,
    At noon or eve we met,
And revelled there in bliss of love
    With evening dewdrops wet;
Beneath the spreading chestnut tree,
    Or where the beech ran high,
With foliage gay, so dear to me,
    Fraught with the wild wind's sigh.

And near us flowed a crystal stream,
    Which murmured music sweet,
And foaming cascade 'neath the beam
    Of sunset, near our feet;
And when the moon's pale lustre shone
    The shadows flitted by
Of those whose day of toil was done,
    Who passed with pensive sigh.

And near us lay the sleeping dead
    In graveyard fresh and green,
The stalwart form, the weary head,
    The clay-cold sod between:
The old church clock oft told the hour
    With half a parting knell,
While Love, with its own magic power,
    Fast bound us with its spell!

And in that grand old church our vow
    Was heard and firmly sealed
One Sabbath morn, as fair as now,
    And mutual love revealed !
Nor years which passed e'er broke the charm
    Which bound us firm through life,
Till chilly Death with potent arm
    Cut short the mortal strife !

Those tender ties are sundered now,
    Though love can never die ;
Cold are those lips and placid brow,
    And ceased that pensive sigh :
They tell me I shall live again
    In union sweet and blest,
Far from the reach of toil and pain,
    Where weary spirits rest !

But rest, alas ! can ne'er be mine
    Whilst storms and tempests blow,
Save when the love and peace divine
    Into this heart shall flow,—
When Hope blooms fair and sheds its ray
    Beyond the silent tomb,
And cloud and mist are chased away,
    And banished far this gloom.

My treasure lies in Heaven above,
    Beyond this changeful sky,
Where every heart beats warm with love,
    And bliss can never die :
When weary is thought's wing for flight
    Through circumambient air,
I look for rest where all is Light,
    And never shadow there !

MISCELLANEOUS.

The Footsteps of Spring.

Swept by an angry gale,
　Torn by the lightning's stroke,
With arms all weary, bent and frail,
Deep in a coppice down the vale
　There stands an aged oak.

But Spring now chains the wind
　And calms the torrent's roar;
The track that Winter leaves behind
She razes with soft hands and kind,
　And lifts the oak once more.

Hard-by a tuneful stream
　Outpours its rippling song,
And lightened gaily by a gleam
Of soft and silvery sunlight beam,
　It swirls and trips along.

Here 'neath a spreading tree
　From out a moss-clad mound,
A pale bud, longing to be free,
Has pushed its head in springtide glee
　Above the silent ground.

There on a leafless limb
　A wee bird twitters low,
Her cup of love full to the brim,
She is not now so shy of him
　Who would a mating go.

    And cheered by warmth and light
      The woodlark soars and sings,
As skyward floating, dim to sight,
A speck outpours its song of might,
      And welkin sweetly rings.

    Now soothing showers descend
      To kiss the blushing land,
While crystal tears and sunlight blend
That brilliant bows may earthward bend,
      All wrought by subtle hand.

    See, as her steps advance,
      In earth and air above,
A thousand pulses lightly dance,
And tones grow soft and soft the glance,—
      She fills the earth with love!

                SAM RICHARDS.

April Night.

    ALL the town is sleeping
      Underneath the hill;
    Only I am keeping
      Restless vigil still.

    Through the day I've waited,
      Still I watch at night:
    Who can tell the fated
      Hour of love-delight?

    All the world is sleeping,
      Fain would I sleep too:
    But my heart wakes, keeping
      Vigil here for you.

                H. D. LOWRY.

The Gorse.

Upon the lonely moorland,
  Ah, what a weary day !
The stream was loud and turbid,
  The sombre sky was grey ;
And though the gorse was golden,
  My love was far away.

Upon the lonely moorland,
  Ah, what a weary day !
The town was grey below me,
  Beyond, the sea was grey ;
And though the gorse was golden,
  My love was far away.

Over the lonely moorland
  There stole at last a ray
Of sunlight through the rifting
  Of sombre clouds and grey ;
Though sun and gorse were golden,
  My love was far away.

Across the barren moorland
  A wandering gleam did play
Upon a cloak of scarlet
  That ever moved my way :
How quick my world grew golden —
  My world that was so grey !

H. D. LOWRY.

The Golden Rule.

Love is the fairest of flowers ;
  Touch it with tenderest hand ;
Nourish its petals with showers
  Till all its beauties expand ;
Breathe its aroma and glory ;
  Scatter its perfume around ;
Sprinkle the locks that are hoary—
  Hearts that with trouble abound.

Learn from Love how to be cheery,
    Guileless, and thinking no ill,
Then, when thy heart is aweary,
    Patience will dwell with thee still;
Comfort the heart in its sorrow;
    Work through Life's vanishing day;
Give, when the needy would borrow,—
    Thou passest but once this way.

Ere thou dost mete condemnation,
    When others' faults are unveil'd,
Banish thy self-adoration,—
    Hast thou not fallen and failed?
Cast out the beam from thy vision;
    Sweeten with honey thy voice;
Speak not with scorn and derision,
    Then will the angels rejoice.

                ANNIE TREVITHICK.

Love's Thoughts.

I think of thee
    As night's soft, filmy veil is drawn aside
    And sunbeams ope day's crimson portals wide;
    In fancy thy fair form is by my side,
    Thy smile is beaming bright, clear as the light,
    Thy face is ever near at early morn.

I think of thee
    When Sol has bathed the earth with golden rays,
    Winning from feather'd choirs their songs of praise;
    Oh, light is labour,—swiftly pass the days;
    With me thou dost abide, tho' seas divide;
    Thinking of thee the hours glide smoothly on.

I think of thee
    When purple shadows creep from out the West,
    And flooding hills and vales. Sol sinks to rest
    As falls a weary child on mother's breast;
    O'er rippling sea thy voice comes back to me
    Through the sweet stillness of calm eventide.

                ANNIE TREVITHICK.

St. Michael's Mount.

MAJESTIC Michael rises—he whose brow
Is crown'd with castles; and whose rocky sides
Are clad with dusky ivy: he whose base,
Beat by the storms of ages, stands unmov'd
Amidst the wreck of things—the change of time.
That base, encircled by the azure waves,
Was once with verdure clad: the towering oaks
Here waved their branches green: the sacred oaks,
Whose awful shades among the Druids stay'd
To cut the hallowed mistletoe, and hold
High converse with their gods.

SIR HUMPHRY DAVY.

Sing, sing, ye Waves, a Requiem!

'Twas a lonely spot, a lonely grave,
   With waving palm trees overhead,—
No sound but the wailing of the wave
   Swept o'er the hapless sleeping dead;
None but the sobbing, sorrowing sea
   Where the wild waves roll eternally.

Sadly and gently they bore him there,
   His mourning comrades rough and brave,
And laid him down with tenderest care
   To rest in that lone foreign grave,
Near the sobbing, sighing, mournful sea
   Where the wild waves roll eternally.

Then back they went to their floating home
   And steered across the treacherous deep,
And left their comrade there alone
   So calmly wrapped in peaceful sleep,
By the sobbing, sighing, mournful sea
   Where the wild waves roll eternally.

No stone doth mark where the sailor lies,
   No teardrops kiss the lonely grave,
But the bending palm there droops and sighs
   And salt tears fall from every wave;
The requiem of a sounding sea
   Is sung by the waves eternally.

                    LENA JORY.

Money: the Modern Idol.

Money! thou god of wondrous power—
Adored in palace, cot, and tower,
   In ships on briny main;
On lofty hills, on fertile lands,
On frozen steppes, on desert sands,
   On mountain and on plain:

Thy worshippers by far exceed
All those of any other creed;
   Thy power none can define;
For Christians, Turks, and Parsees bow
With Buddhists at thy altar low,
   And worship at thy shrine.

Thou nervest for stupendous fight
The strength of Europe's arméd might;
   Thou sett'st the war-fiends free;
The monster gun thy might proclaims
With crashing shock, with smoke and flames:
   Hell's demons laugh with glee.

For love of thee, with bated breath,
The murderer plans his victim's death,
   And strikes the fatal blow;
For love of thee full oft have wed
Youth's downy cheek with hoary head,
   And lived a life of woe.

In deep devotion to thy name
The miser suffers every shame,
   Yet gladdens at thy sight.
By flickering lamp, with bolted door,
He scans thy golden visage o'er
   And chuckles with delight.

He clasps thy form with bony hands;
With joy he kneels, he sits, he stands,
   And capers like a child;
With thee at hand he wants no more:
His lifeless corpse falls to the floor,
   All grim and stark and wild.

Thy magic wand with subtle power
Makes bishops e'en before thee cower,
   With peers and judges grave:
But when stern Death knocks at the door
Thou'rt impotent! Thy power is o'er!
   Thou'rt helpless then to save!

W. F. WOODFIELD.

The Emigrant's Farewell to Mount's Bay.

Farewell, Mount's Bay! A long farewell
  I bid thy rock-bound shore;
My heart nigh breaks with grief to think
  I ne'er may see thee more.

From infancy I've watched thy waves,
  And roamed thy rocks and sands;
But I must leave thee, beauteous bay,
  To toil in other lands.

My heart grows faint—tears blind me so,
  Words fail my love to tell;
My very soul so yearns for thee
  I scarce can say—farewell.

But Manhood bids me dry my tears
  And brace me for the fight;
Adieu, adieu, belovéd bay!
  Farewell, my heart's delight!

                W. F. Woodfield.

The Lake of Killarney.

Oh! let me wander by the lake,
Killarney's sylvan shores;
When warbling high the minstrels wake,
And Sol the heaven soars.

Lo! from the east a glowing light,—
Aurora gilds the main,
While on the hills and rugged height,
The sunbeams dance again.

I've roamed across the mountains,
And through the vernal woods,
I've watched the boiling fountains,
Close by the swelling floods,

Yet I prefer the crystal lake,
With waters ever clear,
And would my native land forsake,
To dwell for ever there.

Yon azure cliffs, majestic high,
Where sea-birds gather round
Beneath a bright autumnal sky,
In echoes now resound.

The startled air and hollow caves
With vocal music ring,—
Born on the breeze across the waves,
Sing on, sweet songsters, sing!

J. F. TIDDY.

The Lizard: An English Lane.

Dear English lane! I love thy bramble walls;
  O'er thee full many a hawthorn flings its shade,
Rolls many a varied leaf that droops and falls
  Across the path by travellers' footsteps made;
Ever the changing winds lift up the boughs
  Made tuneful by the sound of wild bird's trill;
In evening twilight come the gentle cows,
  Long-breathed from panting on the far-off hill.
Yonder the stars of celandine peep out;
  Sweet smiles the pale-eyed primrose on the way;
Hardly the echo brings the distant shout,
  And timid dormice in the hollow play.
Dear lonely lane! who can thy beauties tell
  By morning sun or evening's azure sky?
Or who describe the memories that steal
  Long-rising tears from a late laughing eye,
  To weep for thee and happy days gone by?

AMY OWEN GOOD.

Gone.

Written in 1858.

Mid scenes and haunts of childhood no longer may I tarry,
  Nor joy, nor mirth, can find there any more ;
    The charm of life is gone,
    I'm lone though crowds among,
  And waves a dirge are chanting near the shore.

With spirits blithe and gleesome in youth's heyday we sauntered,
  The songs of warblers fill'd the perfum'd air ;
    Sweetly I pass'd the hours,
    Among the moss and flowers,
  Entwining garlands round her forehead fair.

There's beauty in the flowers, and stars the heavens bespangle,
  Bath'd are the clouds in charming golden sheen ;
    But she was better far
    Than flower, or sun, or star,
  Or brightest galaxy—an angel queen.

When Summer's glow had vanished, and flow'rets fair were faded,
  And snow and hail fell, cov'ring all the plain,
    The music of her voice,
    Made my lov'd home rejoice,
  And seem'd to haste sweet Spring's return again.

But when the days grew longer, and woodlands rang with gladness,
  Into my home came pain and grief and woe ;
    As mists rise from the sod,
    So rose her soul to God,
  And I was left alone to bear the blow.

But still I know her spirit my footsteps e'er is guiding,
  And that both night and day she's always nigh ;
    And ere long I shall be,
    From mundane sorrows free,
  And share her home eternal in the sky.

                        J. Jenkin.

The Silent Tower of Bottreaux.

(A few of the Stanzas.)

The ship rode down, with courses free,
The daughter of a distant sea,
Her sheet was loose, her anchor stored,
The merry Bottreaux bells on board,—
    " Come to thy God in time !"
      Rung out Tintagel's chime,—
    " Youth, manhood, old age, past,
      Come to thy God at last !"

The pilot heard his native bells
Hang on the breeze in fitful swells;
" Thank God !" with reverent brow he cried,
" We make the shore with evening's tide."
    " Come to thy God in time !"
      It was his marriage chime;
    Youth, manhood, old age, past,
      His bell must ring at last !

" Thank God, thou whining knave, on land,
But thank at sea the steersman's hand,"—
The captain's voice above the gale—
" Thank the good ship and ready sail."
    " Come to thy God in time !"
      Sad grew the boding chime;
    " Come to thy God at last !"
      Boom'd heavy on the blast.

Up rose that sea, as if it heard
The mighty master's signal word;
What thrills the captain's whitening lip?
The death-groans of his sinking ship.
    " Come to thy God in time !"
      Swung deep the funeral chime—
    " Grace ! Mercy ! Kindness past,
      Come to thy God at last !"

Still when the storm of Bottreaux's waves
Is waking in his weedy caves,
Those bells, that sullen surges hide,
Peal their deep tones beneath the tide;—
"Come to thy God in time!"
Thus saith the ocean chime;
Storm, billow, whirlwind, past,
"Come to thy God at last!'"

REV. R. S. HAWKER.

Sing! Birdie, Sing!

Sing! Birdie sing! your playmate's abed,
Sing as you ever have sung;
Little list you he is lying there dead,
The string of his life unstrung!

Never again will he welcome your trill
As you wake with the rising sun;
Sing as you may, he for ever is still,
The days of his life are done.

Waits for him only the cold, dark place,
For him waits the massive stone,
How will you fill up his vacant space?
You, in the world, alone!

Sing! Birdie, sing! sing loud and true,
There are others as good as he;
One cloud must not darken the sun for you—
Yours is life; his the grave must be.

There are yet those will love you for his lost sake,
And you, when your race is run,
May-hap with him will your own place take
In the land of the endless sun.

THOMAS CORNISH.

The Smiling Month of May.

TREADING softly o'er the mountains,
  Leaping, dancing on the lea,
Comes the Queen of Months, bestowing
  Blessings bounteous and free;
    School-boys frolic, lambkins play,
    In the smiling month of May.

Like a damsel, decked with jewels,
  Ready for her bridal hour;
Like an angel, clad in brightness,
  Welcomed by each tree and flower,
    Queen of beauty, blithe and gay,
    Comes the smiling month of May.

Lark and linnet haste to meet her;
  Hills and dales rejoice and sing;
Nature chants in adoration;
  Valleys with sweet echoes ring;
    Cuckoo's bell sounds night and day
    In the smiling month of May.

Spring has spread her fresh green mantle;
  Hedges bloom with flowerets wild;
Daisies smile and cowslips ponder,
  As they watch Dame Nature's child:
    Maypole dancers lead the way,
    Welcoming the month of May.

WILLIAM QUINTRELL.

CORNISH DITTIES

BY

GEORGE B. MILLETT,

"The Mayor of Market-Jew."

INTRODUCTORY REMARKS.

MARAZION, or Market-Jew, as it is also commonly called, is a pleasant little town on the northern shore of Mount's Bay, near St. Michael's Mount. No less than seventy different ways of spelling the name occur in various documents.* Marazion was anciently a place of considerable importance, and until as recently as the year 1786 it was the most westerly post town in Cornwall. In very early times much traffic in tin with the Phœnicians was probably carried on here. Hals says that in the time of Henry II. this town was privileged with sending two members to sit in the Commons House of Parliament. Queen Elizabeth granted it a Charter, 13th June, 1795.

After having existed as a Borough for nearly 300 years, Marazion may now no longer claim the privilege, which is swept away under the Municipal Corporations Act, its Corporation being dissolved in 1886. This ditty was written—without the two additional verses—in 1880. "One and All" is the Cornish Motto.

The ordinary white turnips grown in the vicinity are much esteemed for their excellence. Market-Jew turnips are well known. In speaking of fair maids of Market-Jew one is also reminded of "Fumados" the name given to them by Italians—locally called 'Fair Maids," being pressed and salted pilchards, for the preparation of which the fishing towns on the shores of Mount's Bay are noted, large quantities being annually exported to Italy and Spain.

The saying, "standing in his own light, like the Mayor of Market-Jew," is proverbial in the West, having its origin in the fact that in the old chapel (which has given place to the present church), the mayor's seat had a window directly behind it. It is almost unnecessary to state that there is no authority whatever for the assertion that any Mayor of Market-Jew ever so far forgot himself as even to close his eyes in church!

* See "Giano" by R. N. Worth. Trans. Penzance Nat. Hist. and Antiq. Soc. New Series. Vol. II. p. 187.

"The Mayor of Market-Jew."

There's not a town in all the west
    That slopes from waters blue,
By Providence more fully blest,
    Than that of Market-Jew.
For though Penzance I dearly love
    As a Penzance man true,
I'll not forget, where'er I rove,
    I hail from Market-Jew.

For Michael's Mount the place is famed,
    For tin and turnips too,
But greater praise is rightly claimed
    For maids of Market-Jew,
So notable, so good, so fair,
    I'd scarce know where to sue
Had I the chance, yet would I were
    The Mayor of Market-Jew.

A happy man, a rare good man,
    Who nothing has to do,
So right his rule and plain his plan,
    As Mayor of Market-Jew.
Except on Sunday, as is right,
    In church to be on view,
And there he stands in his own light,
    As Mayor of Market-Jew.

And there he sometimes, people tell,
    In state in his own pew,
Sedately sleeps and snores as well,
    As Mayor of Market-Jew.
But worse may ne'er his town befall,
    Nor worse may he do too,
God bless his townsfolk "One and All,"
    And the Mayor of Market-Jew.

*   *   *   *   *

The statement often has been made
    "Corporations do not die,"
But now indeed I'm much afraid
    Its truth we must deny.
Deprived of state, bereft of power,
    Dissolved his council too,
No longer may he strut his hour
    As Mayor of Market-Jew.

So we must bow to powers that be,
    And stifle our regret ;
With other's eyes we'll never see,
    Nor all we wish for get ;
But Market-Jew will still be fair,
    Be loyal, good and true ;
God speed thee, then, without a Mayor,
    Sweet town of Market-Jew.

THE ZENNOR MERMAID.

Written and Composed by George Bown Millett.

'Twas once on a time, ah, long a-go! A youth he lov'd a maid-en so: She was fair as the day, and with golden hair, Long, ah, long a-go!.. But nobody knew from whence she came, Or where she liv'd, or what was her name: They on-ly perceiv'd her di-vine-ly fair, Long, ah, long a-go!..

"[The Zennor Mermaid."

'Twas once on a time, ah long ago,
A youth he loved a maiden so:
She was fair as the day, and with golden hair,
  Long, ah long ago.
But nobody knew from whence she came,
Or where she lived, or what was her name:
They only perceived her divinely fair,
  Long, ah long ago.

The gossips declared she had ill-shapen feet,
She wore such long dresses they could not be neat.
Like a vision she came, and would so disappear,
  Long, ah long ago.
Her rich sunny locks were " too golden," they cried,—
E'en the bloom on her cheeks was carefully eyed:
There was something uncanny about her 'twas clear,
  Long, ah long ago.

'Twas on Sundays alone she ever was seen,
At Zennor Church duly, at morn and at e'en:
Whene'er the bell tolled she was sure to be there,
  Long, ah long ago.
Like an angel she looked, like a nightingale sang,
Through the church the sweet notes of her melody rang,
In exquisite cadence,—'twas music most rare,
  Long, ah long ago.

Now the son of the squire was handsome and tall,
And he long watched the maiden so noticed by all;
But to him she seemed truly like one from above,
  Long, ah long ago.
He oft tried to follow, and find where she went,
But never succeeded,—she foiled his intent;
So he, mutely admiring, fell madly in love,
  Long, ah long ago.

One Sunday it happened she signed to the lad
Ere leaving the church, and it made his heart glad.
He followed, and still she but just kept in sight,
  Long, ah long ago.
Then down to the cove she so quickly repaired,
Whilst he hurried after as quick as he dared,
Till he reached her at last by foaming waves white,
  Long, ah long ago.

'Twas then that she turned, and smiling, said she,
" Come be my dear love, and dwell 'neath the sea,
I've pleasures and riches in deep coral caves."
  Long, ah long ago.
" I'm yours," cried the lad " for ever and aye—
I'll follow wherever you point out the way:"
Then embraced by the Mermaid he plunged in the waves,
  Long, ah long ago.

"Paul Church Town."

SWEET maiden, I pray thee,
One moment oh stay thee,
Canst tell me the way now to Paul Church Town?
I'm listless and dreary,
Foot-sore and weary,
And gladly to-night shall I lay me down:
From trade, streets, and building,
From shops, gas, and gilding,
I seek for seclusion in Paul Church Town.

Keep right up the hill, sir,
But walk with a will, sir,
Lest night should o'ertake you near Paul Church Town,
For such folks as you, sir,
May hap this to rue, sir,
Where pixies in plenty and small folks brown
May lead you astray, sir,
Deceive you till day, sir,
So beware of the pixies near Paul Church Town.

Sweet maid, I beseech thee,
Oh tell me, oh teach me
How best to shun pixies near Paul Church Town.
I'm fearful of danger
Unknown to a stranger,
I've doubts of lone places of such renown,
But if thou would'st guide me
I'd feel safe beside thee,
I'd love thee, I'd wed thee, at Paul Church Town.

You're too fast by half, sir,
I'm not caught with chaff, sir,
Not thus is love made, sir, at Paul Church Town.
I've a husband already
Who's loving and steady -
He's coming I see, sir, the hill-side down,
So quicken your pace, sir,
You can't miss the place, sir,
But beware of the pixies near Paul Church Town.

PRINTED AND PUBLISHED BY F. RODDA, PENZANCE.

www.ingramcontent.com/pod-product-compliance
Lightning Source LLC
Chambersburg PA
CBHW032157160426
43197CB00008B/953